AS YOU ARE

Ignite Your Charisma, Reclaim Your Confidence, Unleash Your Masculinity

NICK SPARKS

Editorial by Joseph J Romm & Tessla Coil

Dedicated to all of my alums for teaching me everything I know about coaching and inspiring the contents of this book. Thank you for putting your faith in me!

Disclaimer

The language I use throughout this book represents men communicating with women because that's what I've successfully taught hundreds of guys to do. My advice, however, applies to anyone, man or woman, who's looking to improve their platonic and romantic communication with anyone else.

Table of Contents

Introduction

I'm a dating coach, but for a long time women were a complete mystery to me.

Some people might find this hard to believe, but the reason I can relate to the hundreds of men with whom I've worked is that at one point or another I had the exact same insecurities that they have now. I've faced every frustration, and thought that things would never get better; I would just have to settle for whatever came to me.

Then, the summer between my sophomore and junior years at the University of Michigan, I rented a room in a house with six sorority girls. I didn't think much of it at the time, but over the course of that summer, as the girls began considering me a friend, I got a glimpse into the female mind that most guys never see.

It really hit me one night, as I was watching American Idol with Ashley and Nicole, when Ashley dropped this bombshell: "Jason is friggin' perfect on paper. He just graduated with a great job at Merrill Lynch. He's nice to me... almost too nice. I *wish* I liked him as much as he likes me, but I just can't get Randy out of my head." "Who is Randy?" I asked, quizzically. "Ugh... He pisses me off. He never calls me back on time. He's charming when he wants to be, and he's not even that hot... but I just CAN'T stop thinking about him. Why am I screwed up, Nick?" she asked me.

That's when I knew my first "theory" about attraction, which had been gaining steam in the back of my mind, was true. Attraction isn't fair. It's not that women don't like nice guys; it's just that women aren't wired the way you've been told. You see, I'd been raised on what I call the "Disney Approach" to attraction -- the lie that if you behave like Prince Charming, put her on a pedestal, do her bidding, and treat her like an all-around princess, then she'll magically fall for you.

Unfortunately, as I'll show you throughout this book, this couldn't be further from the truth. That's the bad news. But I *do* have some good news. Even though attracting women isn't "fair," it can be *simple* when you get just a few crucial things right. If you embody the basic principles I teach you in this book, people will react to you like you're the most awesome guy in the world, and you'll have all the dates with the women you're really attracted to that you could ever want. If you ignore this advice, put this book back on the shelf, and refuse to take action, then you'll keep seeing the same results you've been seeing.

My lesson that evening did not conclude with Ashley's rant about Randy. Soon, Nicole chimed in with, "At least you have someone. I'm smart, I'm cool, I'm hot [she was], why can't I find a guy?"

"Wait a minute," I chimed in, "don't guys try to talk to you all the time?" I had seen it with my own eyes -- some very good looking guys in fact. She replied, "They do, but they're either drunk or they make it all about themselves -- it's desperate."

I could relate to these guys, so I said, "You probably just make them nervous and that's how they compensate." She replied, "Yeah right, they're just cocky assholes, what do they have to be afraid of?"

That hit something I knew to be true: women would never be attracted to a guy who was afraid of them or put them on some pedestal Disney princess style. I knew this, but I still wasn't quite sure how to overcome those insecurities.

Finally, I got to meet, and actually spend quite a bit of time with Randy. Let's just say he wasn't what I was expecting. Ashley wasn't lying when she said he "wasn't that hot." In fact, I'd consider him to be of below average attractiveness, and he even smelled a little bit. I couldn't believe that Ashley was that crazy about him.

I figured Randy must be the most charming, charismatic guy in the world, but he wasn't. He was always cool to me, but he barely said anything. I was used to getting positive responses from people from my sense of humor -- from coming up with something clever to say. Randy just dropped a comment every once in a great while, which I didn't think was all that funny, but would have the women laughing like it was the funniest thing in the world.

There was one thing that set Randy apart: he had the ability to intimidate with just a look. It wasn't aggressive, but it was just enough to make you question yourself a bit. It was more than once that I saw him shoot that look to Ashley before they headed up to her bedroom. I didn't realize it at the time, but I was witnessing an amazing example of the thing that makes the biggest difference in every interaction you have. (Don't worry, I cover it in the first chapter.)

After immersing myself in the female mind that summer and subconsciously picking up some of Randy's mannerisms, I started having more female friends and began dating some pretty amazing girls on campus that fall. My friends who had been absent that summer noticed the difference and began asking for advice. Before long, I became the unofficial coach of the group, which eventually expanded to being the go-to guy around campus for both men and women to come to for dating advice.

Ten years -- and hundreds of clients -- later, I can now see with deadly accuracy all the ways a guy can sabotage his romantic life. Each of my coaching successes and failures have taught me something new, led me to do something a little different, until I reached this point. Now I can teach you the actions needed to turn it all around. Now I can guarantee success.

Can you relate to any of the following guys?

Mateo was sick of being brushed off when he tried to talk to a woman. He didn't know what to say to change this and soon stopped trying to talk to them altogether.

Tony couldn't walk -- and believed that women would never be attracted to a guy in a wheelchair.

David was a lion at getting phone numbers -- but a lamb at getting those women to go on a date.

Adam had trouble telling if a woman was actually into him -- the fact that he was blind didn't help.

Eric was in love with Kaitlin for as long as he could remember, but she didn't see him as anything more than a friend.

While their specific frustrations were different, these men all had one thing in common: they were unsatisfied with their dating lives or social lives in general. They didn't want to settle, face a messy divorce, pass their insecurities down to their children, or limit their professional development. They had tried to change things in the past, failed, and began to wonder if they could change. Deep down though, they had a feeling that they deserved better.

This is the reason that these men and hundreds of others from all over the globe choose to work with me -- well, that and my 100% satisfaction rate.

I'm a dating coach. It's my job to resolve these frustrations, give guys complete confidence with women, and deliver the life we all truly deserve -- amazing friends, a lack of anxiety when it comes to social and sexual communication, and the prospects of a partner who we're truly excited to be with.

A lot of people, especially women, are surprised that my job exists -- women often think we men have it relatively easy. I've heard this complaint from many female friends: "I have to sit and wait for a guy to approach me. You can talk to whomever you want." But in a culture where men are told since birth that any expression of our sexual interest in women is "creepy," where formal education on romance is done by Disney, my job turns out to be in high demand.

Most guys think it's impossible to completely transform themselves in just 72 hours into charismatic Don Juans who radiate confidence. Yet that's exactly what I help my clients do, weekend after weekend.

I highlight all the things that an individual does to sabotage himself from being his most charismatic self in the interactions he cares most about. We've all been, "on," socially, in our lives, and we've all faltered under pressure -- I teach you to be the former all the time, especially when it matters most. Follow this advice, and magically, people start reacting to you differently.

The first day you put it into practice, you'll notice people responding more strongly to you, with more energy and enthusiasm. You'll still be wondering if it can be this easy, and you'll still stumble here or there. The second day, your coworkers will start to tell you there's something different about you -- that they can't quite put their finger on it but you're not the same person.

By the fifth day -- just five days from now! -- EVERYONE in your life is going to be treating you differently. That's the other reason why my success rate is unparalleled: If you just tried to practice these skills the few times you were around a woman you liked, you'd still be terrible, especially around the people who intimidate you the most. But these skills are universal, and you should be applying them with every person you come into contact with. In every conversation you have you're strengthening your new skills or going on 'autopilot' and reinforcing self-sabotaging behaviors.

Soon, your friends will be showing you more respect, your office crush will be coming by your cubicle to start up conversations, and you'll be more impressive in job interviews and have greater professional success.

If all you want to do is have more options in your dating life -- or have a lot more great sex (or any at all) -- this book will certainly deliver. But if you are like most of the guys I coach, you want something more.

You've felt something inside of you for a while now – an inner self who has been afraid, who has held back, who could be so much more attractive and confident if you only had the tools to unlock it within yourself. And that's what this book is *really* all about:

- Finding that powerful, confident, fearless self who knows he can be so much more

- Discovering the natural voice inside you that attracts people without even trying

- Knowing that you never have to worry about this stuff again for the rest of your life -- that you've got it handled

I'm going to spend the next 120 pages teaching you the same set of social skills that my clients pay $3000 to learn over the course of 3 days and nights. Before you flip ahead to whatever area is the most intriguing to you though, I want to make one thing clear:

If you just read a book on playing piano or tennis, you're not going to become a much better piano or tennis player. Similarly, if you just read this book but don't dedicate yourself to taking the simple actions I prescribe, you won't see any dramatic differences in your life.

It sounds easy, but the actions I prescribe will make you feel uncomfortable, not only because you don't do them often, but because they force you to confront your insecurities and all of the mixed messages that our culture has provided.

It's straightforward, but it's not easy -- changing your life never is and anyone who promises otherwise is lying.

Before you turn the page, think about whether or not you're living the life that you really want. I always say, "I can show you the path, but you have to walk it." Now is the time to decide if you're ready to walk that path and earn the life you always dreamed of.

If not, no worries -- it's a big step and not everyone is ready for it. But if you're ready to break free from your current trajectory and fight for what you really want, then keep reading.

SECTION ONE

How to Start Interactions Fearlessly

CHAPTER 1

The Only Thing That Matters
When You Start a Conversation

Starting conversations with strangers isn't a necessary skill in today's day and age -- especially when it comes to dating. Given the proliferation of online dating and dating apps, or even an old-fashioned introduction from a friend, you could meet the woman of your dreams without ever having to say "hi" to a stranger.

But what if you move to a new town and are suddenly no longer surrounded by your old friends? What if you go to a party and want to meet new people? What if you're at a networking event and your future professional prospects are determined by your ability to meet and greet? While being able to start a conversation with strangers certainly isn't a *necessary* skill, it's not difficult to argue that your life can be greatly enhanced by acquiring it.

The first time I met Mateo, I was a little intimidated. Although I saw right off that he was an awesome guy, at that point in time I had no experience with speech impediments, and he had a very strong stutter.

The very first night, however, it became clear why Mateo was having trouble -- and it wasn't directly because of his stutter. When he tried to start conversations with people he was hesitant, almost apologetic. He left the impression, "I don't mean to bother you," without even saying it. As a result, people would get the feeling that he was bothering them and blow him off.

15

It wasn't the stutter that was holding Mateo back; it was the way that he had adapted to past hurts and experiences. These defense mechanisms may have made him feel safe for a time, but were now creating a life he was unsatisfied with. Because of the responses he had gotten to his stutter in the past he withdrew. And when he did approach strangers, he would keep his eyes down, stay at an awkward distance, and speak in hushed, timid tones. His actions, borne of fear, were creating the negative responses he was getting.

The secret to starting conversations is that no one can blow you off unless you let them. If you come in apologetically -- unsure of yourself and looking for validation from people to let you know that you're okay -- then you are likely to get dismissed. If you act like an annoying fly buzzing around, then it's only a matter of time before people swat you away. If you come in with a strong presence, sure of your actions, and present yourself in a way that deserves attention, then it will be nearly impossible for people to brush you away.

Within the first 5 to 10 seconds of meeting you, people have already formed their judgments about you. Other than their own mood at the time and your instant mutual chemistry, the only thing that this judgment is based off of is *your ability to hold space.*

Think back to the last time you had a conversation with a woman who made your heart beat faster. Really remember what she looked like; think of every single detail you can recall from the interaction. Do you remember how nervous she made you feel?

Now, imagine you had looked her in the eye and held her stare. Imagine neither of you said anything in that moment, and instead just let the tension build between you. How do you feel now? Are there words to describe it?

I use an example that evokes more extreme emotion, however human beings are always feeling something, and proximity to other human beings affects those feelings. When one person looks at another person they both feel something else. When they look at each other different feelings are evoked. When they move closer to one another, when they communicate with one another, if there's mutual attraction ... these all send different combinations of feelings through each person.

Whenever we interpret these feelings as nervousness for whatever reason, human beings tend to fall back onto comfortable behavioral patterns that may have helped them alleviate those feelings at one time, but now only block their ability to communicate those feelings and act honestly upon them in that moment.

Holding space is simply allowing those feelings to arise and listening to them rather than running away from them by cycling through personal social avoidance mechanisms -- or as I call them, "ruts."

Mateo's ruts may have been a little deeper because of the shame he'd internalized over the stutter, but we all have them. I'll be detailing them, and how to overcome them, in the following chapters, but the most common ruts can be summarized as retreating into one's head and overanalyzing the situation or getting jittery and talking too much. In both of these cases, their eye contact gets erratic and they're clearly not present in the moment. All of these things combine to make women (or anyone you're speaking with, for that matter) feel uncomfortable.

It's no different than if you were building a home. You go to the first contractor's office, and it happens to be his first week working at this particular firm. He's a bit nervous -- unsure about how exactly the process works, anxious to prove himself at this new job, over-excited because you're his first customer -- and it shows. You don't know why he's nervous, but you definitely feel uncomfortable. You may guess that he's pondering his compensation package or perhaps trying to rip you off. Of course, he's just anxious to please you, but you don't know that -- all you know is that something doesn't feel right.

Then you go to the second contractor's office. He happens to have the same amount of experience as the other contractor, but has stayed at the same firm for his whole career. As a result, he's comfortable in his environment and secure in his knowledge of the process. He is calm and attentive, listening to your needs and making expert recommendations. His confident attitude puts you at ease. You feel relaxed because he does. When he looks you in the eye and tells you that it's all going to be taken care of, you believe him, and that's who builds your house.

It's the same feeling you get when you're going about your day, but you take a minute to focus on the server, barista, cashier, etc., and ask them honestly how they're doing -- not with the robotic pleasantries we all spit out on autopilot or with some agenda to get something from them, but pausing to look them in the eye and showing that you genuinely feel interested in what is going on in their life. The words don't matter. What matters is the truth of your feelings. When you feel that genuine emotion behind your communication, I'm sure you've noticed that they almost always respond positively and with a bit of surprise, since they're not used to meeting people who care.

When you look another person in the eye, a lot of feelings emerge. This moment can be called the "moment of truth" because in that instant, they are both aware of what the other person is feeling (at least subconsciously). When close friends find themselves in an interesting situation they'll often look each other in the eye to get a sense for where the other person is at.

Sharing one's eye contact and the full range of feelings behind it with someone says, "I'm ok with myself, how are you?" This was the only "power" Randy had back in college: he was comfortable with himself, a feeling otherwise known as confidence. The reason why I felt intimidated by his eye contact wasn't because it was inherently intimidating, but rather because his comfort with himself reflected my own lack of confidence. Not feeling comfortable enough to share your eye contact while being present with your feelings can be interpreted as shy, not interested in opening up, or hiding something. Either way, when a person jumps into a rut at this point instead of communicating their underlying feelings vulnerably the move toward greater intimacy is immediately halted.

That feeling, be it the tension arising when you and a woman to whom you're attracted look each other in the eye, the trust that makes you settle on that contractor, or the genuine feeling that lets the server know you really care, is the most important aspect of all human communication. Without it, we're just computers sending data, and our conversations are meaningless. With it, they're all meaningful, regardless of what is said. If you're holding that space and allowing the natural feelings to arise rather than retreating into haphazard thoughts and empty words, the other person will feel what you're saying, and you'll be communicating in the most attractive way possible.

A common issue I get asked about is how a guy will feel lost when trying to interact with a group, whether it be a group of women at a social function or a group of colleagues in the conference room. The secret is taking a moment to hold space when communicating with each person of the group, rather than trying to talk to everyone at once. If you try to talk to everyone, you're actually talking to no one and you'll soon be ignored by the group or interrupted. If instead you are fully emotionally present as you speak to one person at a time you'll not only capture the other person's attention, but the attention of the moment for the rest of the group as well.

If you catch yourself falling back into your old ruts and getting into your head or talking haphazardly that's fine. You're improving at becoming more aware of your tendencies and what situations evoke them, which is always the first step. Give those tendencies a quick hug because they've helped you in the past -- then quickly brush them off like a snowflake and refocus your attention on the feelings of the moment.

Note: if you try this only with the women who make you nervous and allow your old behaviors to govern all other interactions, then you will never truly improve, nor will others' responses to you. Whenever you're not focusing on holding space, you're probably falling back into your old ruts and patterns and reinforcing those self-sabotaging actions even more. If you're not consciously forcing yourself to perform this vital but under-practiced skill with everyone, then you're just continuing on your current trajectory.

As you emerge from auto-pilot and begin holding space with every person you encounter, your skills will get better -- and so will the way people feel about and respond to you. While it may be scary and nerve-wracking being that vulnerable at first, the stronger your muscles get and the more positive interactions you have, the easier it will be for you to do it well. Practicing holding space with anyone and everyone you come across, and with yourself, is how you achieve mastery and reroute the path of your life.

***

While holding space is the most important social skill you can ever develop -- the foundation for everything else I discuss in this book -- there is one other thing that's equally important when starting conversations with strangers, at least in a social setting.

To return to our friend Mateo, although his interactions with one or two people began improving as he practiced holding space, whenever he tried to enter a conversation with a group of people, he still felt like the odd man out. This fear was confirmed as they physically shut him out of the group time and time again. Watching him, though, it was clear that they weren't making him the odd man out -- he was doing it to himself with nothing more than a half-step.

As I observed Mateo approach group after group from my vantage, it couldn't have been clearer. Everyone else in the group held a similar distance from each other -- a friendly distance that we normally take when interacting with people with whom we're comfortable. When Mateo approached though, he was keeping himself about a half-step farther away from everyone else. It's another common rut -- when we're further away from everyone it doesn't feel as awkward to us. This half-step, however, creates an awkward distance for everyone else that screams, "I'm an outsider; I'm not one of you."

Presenting himself as an outsider guaranteed that the group would feel the nervousness he was bringing, judge him as such, and with the distance he created it was easy for the rest of them to shut him out of the circle. I had him focus on moving in that extra half-step to make himself a part of the group when he approached and immediately he noticed a big change. Now that he was standing at normal distance, the other people stopped viewing him as an outcast and started treating him as a member of the group. Although the intimacy brought on by the added closeness felt scary as all heck to Mateo at first, it quickly became comfortable -- not in the same "safe" way that it was before, but in the way it felt when he was with friends. He no longer got shut out because he no longer invited people to shut him out.

For guys who have the issue of distance, they feel as though they're plenty close, even though they're actually this half step away. I'll say, "Get closer", and they reply, "How much closer do you want me to go?" Often, it won't be until I can show them an example of someone else trying to talk to women at an awkward distance -- easy to find at almost any bar -- that they start to get an idea of where they're going wrong.

***

Notice that in discussing the elements of an attractive approach I didn't make one mention of the words you use. That's because, at least in the first five to ten seconds, they don't matter. Her disposition aside, if you've got the most charming opening line in the world but you deliver it weakly, you'll probably get a negative response. But in a social situation you can say nothing more than, "Hey [pause] how's it going?" slowly, while holding space and being vulnerable with your feelings through your eye contact, and probably get a positive response. This is why the old excuse, "I wanted to talk to her but I couldn't think of anything to say," is so weak. The words never mattered in the first place.

Guys who are comfortable with women don't ever worry about what they're going to say. They simply say "hi" while making great eye contact, fully comfortable with themselves, and know that some women will be open to interacting further and some won't. The goal of starting conversations with strangers shouldn't be to get a positive response, it should simply be to find out who's interested in talking more -- and who isn't.

As expected, over the course of the weekend, the responses Mateo received from women became drastically better -- but a totally unexpected occurrence surprised everyone. As Mateo stopped worrying about the response he'd get, and started showing up confidently, his stutter began to disappear. He started smiling more, which was especially nice because he had a bright, genuine smile that made everyone around him feel better. By the end of the weekend, the stutter was almost gone, and I could barely recognize the new man who would light up almost anyone he approached.

One of the things Mateo learned that weekend was a lesson I hope every one of my clients takes away from working with me: you can be ignored only if you let yourself. You can blame a stutter, or being short, or anything else that you want to use as an excuse -- but it's your actions that create your life. Whether it's a first date, a business meeting, holding a conversation, or getting more sexual, allowing your -- and everyone else's -- genuine feelings to be expressed instead of avoiding and twisting them through your fears is the most valuable skill you will ever learn. Holding space creates human communication. With it, you possess the secret of the universe. Without it, you're just talking at people.

Principle 1: Hold Space With Everyone and Identify Your Ruts

CHAPTER 2

How to Always Get "In the Zone"

Before that fateful summer changed my perception of women forever, I noticed something odd. During most of my freshman and sophomore years of college, as I mentioned, women seemed like an alien species to me (thanks *Women Are From Venus!*). But on very rare occasions, maybe once or twice a semester, I was just "on." Everyone I talked to seemed to light up at my presence. It seemed as though every woman I talked to was attracted to me. I still had no idea what to do next, so I fumbled away most of those potential connections, but that was the first time I began to suspect that I could enjoy those kinds of interactions anytime. I figured I was onto something when my friends reported similar results.

Just about all of us have had times in our lives when we were just on, socially. Maybe it was at some party -- a few drinks were probably involved -- but the normal hesitation we usually feel when it comes to talking to strangers seemed to magically disappear. Not only was it easy to start conversations, but other people seemed to enjoy our company and react to us more strongly than usual.

Can you picture at least one moment in your life when you were in this zone? Now, what if I told you that you had the power to get there and enjoy social interactions that way anytime you chose, and that doing so was no more complicated than flicking on a light switch? Luckily for all of us, it couldn't be more true.

As I started working with more and more clients, I noticed that if their first or second interactions went well then that pattern would almost always continue. They would naturally start doing the things we were working on. But if the first or second interactions didn't go so well, it was much more difficult for me to keep them from falling back into their ruts.

This pattern repeated itself so many times I began to call it "social momentum." The idea behind social momentum is analogous to Newton's First Law of Motion: an object in motion will stay in motion and an object at rest will stay at rest -- unless affected by some outside force.

Once we're "in motion" socially, we become more present, holding space and enjoying the moment, and it becomes easier to initiate great conversations. When we're "at rest," it's difficult to stay out of our head unless some other force interferes. Those nights when you were just "on," the reason you got to that place was because some outside force got your social momentum rolling. Maybe a friend introduced you to someone new or you happened to bump into a more social person in some interesting situation, and a conversation was unavoidable.

The longer you're at a venue without talking to new people, however, the more difficult it becomes to do so, and the more awkward you'll appear if you eventually do. If I attend a social event and my social momentum doesn't get rolling in the first hour or two I'm probably getting to bed early because I'd probably enjoy a good night's rest more than standing around and trying to fumble through awkward conversations. If I want to have a good time though, and not leave it up to a friend's introduction or a Hollywood style "meet cue," then that force that gets me in motion has to be my own willpower and the actions I myself take.

With that in mind, here are some actions I take to get my social momentum rolling:

MAKE IT A HABIT

If you don't regularly start conversations with strangers, then it will be nearly impossible to gracefully do so in an intimidating venue, especially with someone who makes your heart beat faster. If you want to be able to say something to a stranger at a party while holding space and without fumbling over your words, then you have to do so with the guy at the bus stop and the elderly woman at the grocery store. The trick is to make saying something more common than not.

Again, your goal isn't to get a positive response, it's merely to express your feelings at the moment and see if they're in the mood to socialize or not.

TALK TO A STRANGER AS SOON AS POSSIBLE

If I want to socialize with people I don't already know, I try to get my social momentum rolling as soon as possible. After spending some time enjoying friends' company, I'll usually go to the bar (typically where people are most open to socializing with strangers), order a drink, and force myself to say something to whoever is next to me while focusing on holding space. If it's a party or networking event and there's no bar then most new conversations still start around the place where refreshments are served. If someone new happens to come around while I'm socializing with friends, that's even better. Most people want to socialize in those situations but are just as nervous as you are. Someone has to say "hi" first.

It doesn't matter who they are. If they look at least a little bit interested in talking I'll say something. I'll acknowledge that at first I'm still "at rest" (my most stiff and awkward disposition) and therefore not expecting fireworks (if they happen even better), and simply try to enjoy the interaction as much as possible while avoiding my own ruts.

The real point of this is to kill the monster known as hesitation. The second you feel like you want to say something to someone you don't know, the vast majority of the time you'll start to feel some hesitation. Your muscles will begin to tense and every plausible (yet fallacious) excuse for inaction will begin to run through your mind. This is a perfectly natural reaction, but one that will consistently sabotage you if you allow it to run your life.

Women can sense hesitation a mile away, and it's always a turnoff. You've heard women like confidence -- well, that's the opposite of not being comfortable expressing your feelings. For every second you hesitate, even if you do manage to say something, your muscles will be more tense, you'll be more in your head, your eye contact will be dodgier – ruts, ruts, ruts. The women will almost always feel you lurking off to the side, feel your hesitation, and become instantly less interested in talking to you.

While you're still more likely to enjoy a great interaction than not if you say "hi" no matter how long you wait beforehand, every moment you hesitate makes it more likely that you'll never get the opportunity to shine. On Thursday, the first night of my weekend clinic, I expect hesitation. By Saturday night I expect it to be overcome. It'll still pop up from time to time, but the more quickly you conquer it, the easier it becomes to do so and the less often it appears in every aspect of your life.

BRING ON THE SMALL TOWN CHARM

In a big city, people tend to walk around as if they're wearing blinders, ignoring those around them. If you've ever lived in or visited a small town, however, you've experienced a very different reality. In these quaint situations, it's more common than not for people to greet each other with a smile, a nod, and warm greeting wherever they are.

Although this small town charm is hard to find in most well-populated areas, if you make it a point to greet everyone you encounter with this warmth, not only will you make other people's day better, but you'll feel better as well. I like to say that every positive response you receive is worth ten passive/negative responses in terms of social momentum. Thus, every time you encounter someone and don't attempt to share some warm feelings, you're missing an opportunity to develop your holding space muscles, develop your social momentum muscles, and make everyone's day a little brighter. Plus, it's not uncommon for these warm greetings to turn into full blown conversations if one of you takes a little more initiative.

FIND A FRIENDLY PERSON

Feelings are contagious, and if I'm still feeling a little "stiff" then nothing would get me out of my shell (protecting me from being vulnerably present in the moment) more than someone whose social momentum is already rolling. Maybe it won't be the first, second, or third person I talk to, but if I really want to meet new people then at first I'm almost on a hunt: "Who can I enjoy a fun interaction with?!"

Once I've had one of these interactions it's almost impossible not to feel great, and from there on out you're less and less hesitant with every positive interaction. You are less fazed by any of the passive/negative reactions you do get from people who aren't yet in the mood to socialize. Better still, the stronger your momentum is the more likely they'll "catch" your feelings and begin to have more fun themselves.

The ability to get your social momentum going is a muscle. The more you do it, the easier it is to get yourself into "the zone" whenever you'd like, while the less you do it, the more difficult it becomes. Developing this ability is straightforward to do, but it isn't easy. None of the most important skills in life ever are.

Principle 2: Make Socializing a Habit and Get Your Social Momentum Rolling ASAP

CHAPTER 3

The Secret to (Almost) Never Getting Rejected

On my first night out with Michael I noticed that upon entering a bar, he would always approach the woman he was most attracted to first. His social momentum was non-existent, so he was at his most awkward, and yet he tried to talk to the woman who made him the most nervous. Even when he assured me that he was "fine" and "not nervous at all" -- even when he approached them with confidence and without hesitation -- the woman could still tell that he was completely in his head and projecting an anxious vibe. Naturally, the woman would be much more likely to politely or impolitely ask him to leave. But because he was attracted to her, he was more likely to take it personally, starting a downward spiral of frustration that was impossible to hide. As his disposition soured, it created worse and worse responses from everyone he attempted to talk to.

Your first goal when you go out should be to get your social momentum rolling, as I previously discussed. Instead of looking for with the women I happen to find most attractive, I first pay attention to the people who are out to socialize. This may be a bit difficult if you're not sure what to look for, but fortunately it's much easier to notice when you're not centering your evaluation of others around their looks as Michael did.

Let's be clear, though, a quick glance isn't enough to read a situation. To learn where a person is at, you must spend a little time holding space while you take her in so you can get a *feel* for where she's at.

While a person's possible dispositions are as numerous as the stars, I've found that they can be broken down into three categories for the purpose of socializing:

The first type is "she wants you to talk to her." A woman might glance or look directly at you, projecting a feeling of openness.

Maybe she holds space with you when you make eye contact, returns your small town warmth, and holds space with you for a moment or two -- the signal can't get much stronger than that. Maybe she catches your eyes, looks away nervously like you often do when you're intimidated by a woman, and then peeks back at you and smiles nervously. The peek-back is adorable and immediately puts a smile on my face -- it's like I caught her checking me out -- and I definitely hold space and look her in the eyes while I'm smiling so she can feel my genuine appreciation. Sadly, most guys miss this because they look away when she does. NEVER MISS A PEEK-BACK!

Unfortunately, many women have been told repeatedly that they shouldn't initiate conversation with a guy they like -- the man is traditionally expected to be the aggressor. So when you get this type of eye contact it's the equivalent of her holding up a sign that says, "PLEASE COME TALK TO ME". When I see this and I want to talk to her, I'll almost always excuse myself from my friends and make a bee-line in her direction (unless I'm in the middle of a serious conversation).

Someone with this disposition is almost guaranteed to be open to conversing, and these interactions can create fireworks. Note that the more you're having a good time socializing in a venue, the more you're going to see these looks.

The second category is what I refer to as "looking to socialize." Sometimes people go out to catch up with friends, sometimes they go out to mix and mingle. You can identify the latter group by their behavior. They are noticeably looking around hoping to catch eye contact or something exciting going on, they're greeting with some "small town charm," they're speaking a little (or a lot) more loudly than those around them, and they're radiating more energy than the people around them. Maybe it's an entire group, maybe it's just one or two individuals in a group. When I see people with this disposition I know that I'd probably have a great time getting to know them at the very least.

I call the third and final category, "what have you got to lose?" Maybe they're deeply into their own conversation and aren't looking around at all. Maybe they catch your eye and then look away with nary a peek-back. Either way, they aren't giving you any outward signal of interest in socializing, but they're not sending off a "please leave me alone" vibe either. Now maybe they're actually not interested in socializing, or maybe they're just shy. While your improving ability to be present with the feelings of the moment should help you guess more accurately, *you can never know for sure unless you say "hi".*

I've seen people who seemed totally uninterested in socializing just light up when a client says something to them. They were out to socialize but were just shy. I've also seen a group of "what have you got to lose?" turn into "looking to socialize" after twenty minutes and a lap on the dance floor.

Keep in mind that people with this third disposition won't be open to socializing as often as the first two, but if you're not seeing either of those, well, then you've got nothing to lose by saying "hi" and seeing if they're in the mood to socialize -- and maybe great connection is just beyond.

The bottom line: **Communication starts before words are ever spoken.** To give yourself the best chance of getting your social momentum going and having a great time, spend some time getting a feel for where everyone is at. Talk to people who want to talk to people, don't miss a peek back, and try not to start your night talking with people who aren't giving off the vibe that they want to talk to strangers -- but don't write them off either.

By Saturday night Michael had learned to read a room, and he took physical attraction off the pedestal. He didn't have to worry about "rejection" because he was paying attention to the communication happening before words were ever spoken. He started by talking with the people who were obviously there to socialize. As his social momentum got rolling during an interaction that he was obviously enjoying the heck out of, he noticed a woman who really made his heart beat faster checking him out. As his conversation wore down he exchanged phone numbers with new friends, politely excused himself from that group, approached that woman and ended up having his best connection of the entire weekend.

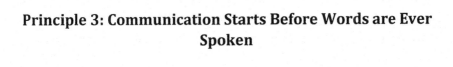

Principle 3: Communication Starts Before Words are Ever Spoken

----

CHAPTER 4

The Best 7 Opening Lines. Period.

Mateo would often blame the problems he was having starting conversations on "not knowing what to say." As I mentioned in the first chapter, that's a common excuse among guys I work with. But after I coached him to hold space, get his social momentum going, and read a room, he saw for himself that "not knowing what to say" was a red herring.

Of course, you have to say something to start a conversation. But everything I say is dead simple and easy to pull out of my back pocket at a moment's notice. Why? If I'm trying to remember some line or just spewing out the same thing out for the hundredth time it's impossible for me to be present, hold space, and communicate any genuine feeling in the moment.

Even if I said something once that got an insane response because of how intensely I was feeling what I said in that moment -- if I tried to say the same thing in a different situation that insane response wouldn't happen because it wasn't genuine. Instead, my focus is on holding space, noticing who's interested in socializing, and saying the first thing off the top of my head.

With this in mind, here are the ways I've found myself starting a conversation 95% of the time:

EYE CONTACT

Sharing eye contact while being vulnerable with one's feelings is the main way human beings nonverbally start conversations. Sometimes that conversation is friendly, sometimes it's aggressive, sometimes it's anxious, but that first look typically dictates the rest of the conversation.

A natural defense mechanism that human beings possess is to "feel" when someone else is looking at us. I'm sure you've had moments when you a got a funny sensation and looked over your shoulder to catch someone else looking back at you. Sending this feeling is a non-verbal way to say, "hey," to someone.

If you're at a crowded bar and want to get a drink you can use this knowledge to your advantage. Square your shoulders up to the bar and clear out your mind as much as possible -- focusing only on the bartender and the feelings of the moment. You'll often notice a little shift when they feel your gaze, and more times than not the next person the bartender will look at will be you -- just be sure to have your drink order ready. I've won several drinks using this knowledge on bets with women who didn't think it was possible for a guy to get a drink from a male bartender before an attractive woman.

With this knowledge, I'll take my time getting a sense of where a person is at with curious interest until she looks in my direction, or looks away with a "not interested in socializing" vibe. Once again, I'm just saying "hey" without words. If her response indicates she wants me to talk to her (don't forget to wait for peek backs!) then I smile and say hi immediately. If I don't do anything when she looks back at me with any sort of openness and just keep staring, then she'll begin wonder why I'm staring and feel creeped out, just like if you said "hey" to someone and didn't say anything else. Saying something just confirms that you were just looking at her because you were interested in socializing with her.

Also, because this approach involves the confident emotional vulnerability of great eye contact, it's more attractive than any verbal communication ever could be. That being said, you eventually have to say something. Here's what I've found to most often come from my mouth in those situations.

"HEY, HOW'S IT GOING?"

In situations where she's giving me "please talk to me" eye contact, and I'm more nervous, and it's difficult for me to think of much else, this is usually the first thing that comes out of my mouth. It's short, sweet, and tells a woman, "I'm comfortable with myself, I don't feel like I have to put on a show to impress you, and I'm interested in you." These things, along with the slight bit of mystery that follows this approach -- who is this guy and how is he so confident? -- are almost universally attractive.

This approach also exemplifies how important it is to be present in the moment. If I mumble "Hey, how's it going," with weak eye contact and awkward distance due to being in my head, or blare fake confidence and interest while subconsciously signaling that I'm still in my head, I'll probably get blown off a moment later. If I say "Hey" with a presence that deserves attention, look her in the eye while holding space, and pause for a moment or three before saying "How's it going?" in a way that lets her know I actually care, the other person is 99% more likely to want to talk to me.

WE'RE ALL FRIENDS

This one has two variations that are based on the same principle -- that we're all already friends. The first variation is what I call "joining conversations." As the name implies, if I happen to overhear something from a neighboring conversation and I can relate to it in any way I'll say something as if I were already part of the conversation. Are they talking about a movie? I'll throw in my thoughts on that movie or ask how it was if I was thinking about seeing it. From the Midwest? We're basically family. While holding space is still most important, this approach almost always seems to be well received.

The other side of the "we're all friends" coin is to bring a passerby into your conversation. If I'm saying something to my friends and a stranger walking past catches my eye, I'll turn towards her and finish my statement as if she were a part of our conversation, often immediately followed by a "you know?" Often she'll just smile and keep walking to wherever she was headed in the first place -- a person in motion tends to stay in motion -- but there's also a good chance that she'll be intrigued and stop and join you. It's always worth a shot, because even if she keeps walking to join her friends she's more likely to want to talk with the social, outgoing guy later on.

SHARED EXPERIENCE

This one is easy, and I'm sure you've done it before. When you and another person are both sharing the same experience, make a comment on it. It could be that it's taking forever to get a drink at a busy bar, a guy is doing something absurd on the train, or you're both checking out the same books at a bookstore. Whatever the shared experience is, saying something about it will almost always yield a welcome response.

SHERLOCK HOLMES COMPLIMENTS

Sherlock Holmes' talent, which made him such an amazing detective (other than incredible deductive reasoning), was to notice the little details that most people miss. While I'm observing what kind of mood someone's in, I'm also noticing those little details in what they're wearing or how they're acting that usually go unnoticed by most people. Then I express my feelings.

People, and especially women, are sick of generic compliments because they know they're insincere, but they love attention to detail. For example, "Nice shirt" will almost always get met with a well deserved roll of her eyes, whereas "All of the colors on your shirt are really exciting" will almost always get a positive response (as long as you actually feel that way). Similarly, "Cool purse" is alright, but "Your purse looks like a disco ball" sets you apart from every other guy.

Maybe it's the fact that he's wearing a shirt for a band you love or that she put in the consideration to match her eyeliner to her outfit -- if you comment on these things, and even more so demonstrate how they make you feel, then you're going to stand out.

NOTICING SOMETHING INTERESTING

Wherever we went, my grandmother would share whatever was on her mind with whoever was around. She was definitely someone who made socializing a habit and never suffered for friends!

If we were at the grocery store and the broccoli was on sale, she'd probably mention it to anyone nearby. Sometimes the other person would just smile politely, and sometimes they'd be off talking for awhile, extending my trip to the grocery store for another 10 minutes.

See something that surprises you? Maybe ribeyes are on special at the grocery store that week, or maybe the muffins at the coffee shop look extra appealing that day. Whatever it is, share it with someone around you.

POSITIVE FEELING

Feeling good about something in the moment? Has the weather just turned amazing? Love the song that's playing? Just tasted the most delicious drink you've ever had in your life? Be sure to share these things with the person next to you. Nine people out of ten will appreciate the ray of sunshine.

***

That's it. That's really about all that you'll ever need to start great conversations, not counting all the other random things that pop into your head in the moment. I can't stress enough that it's not what you say, but how you say it, and that you're not attempting to win a woman over, you're merely checking to see whether she is in the mood to have an enjoyable conversation. If you have some agenda and only try to do this with women you're attracted to, most people won't respond well to you. If you make it a habit to say whatever's on your mind to whoever's next to you -- while holding space so that it can be delivered with genuine emotion and great eye contact -- then they'll probably respond positively.

Now that you've got some examples of what you can say and the reasons why they don't really matter, you don't have any excuses for not saying something if you want to socialize. It really is as simple as walking up and saying, "hi."

Make saying the first thing that comes to your mind to everyone you come across a habit, and after becoming empowered by all of the positive responses you get, your troubles with approaching strangers will be only a memory.

Principle 4: Say Whatever's on Your Mind to Whoever's Around You

----

CHAPTER 5

The Sentence That Destroys "Rejection"

Before Mateo became an approaching wizard, he would take a woman's passive or negative reactions personally and let them ruin his entire evening. Even though I explained to him that her reaction has more to do with her disposition than anything about him personally, it's one thing to believe it intellectually and another to feel it when she's rolling her eyes.

No matter how hard you try to fight it, those negative reactions -- which are as inevitable as the rain -- can throw you off and sabotage the rest of your day or night. For this reason, I teach what I call the "warm goodbye," a simple sentence that reminds you of your power in that moment and allows you to exit any situation gracefully. The warm goodbye grounds your feelings in what you already know intellectually -- that she's not "rejecting" you, she's just not in the mood to socialize right now and/or there's a rut you can become more aware of.

When she demonstrates she's not in the mood to socialize the worst thing you can do is put your head down and silently slink away. This just confirms every insecurity in your head – *she didn't like me and I wasn't good/attractive/charming enough for her – in short, I got rejected (again).* And everyone watching the event gets the same impression: that guy was shot down hard.

Instead of putting your head down and giving in to your worst fears in this moment, it's instead time to employ what I call the warm goodbye. With a warm smile on your face, simply say some version of, "It's been a pleasure talking with you. Have a great night."

While unassuming on the surface, this simple sentence does three powerful things:

1. It makes her rethink her actions

If you try to awkwardly drag out a conversation that she's clearly not interested in having, ignoring basic social protocols before slinking away awkwardly, then you just validated her actions. She was cold to you because you were being weird. If instead you expertly assess her situation and excuse yourself with the warm goodbye, then she may instead think something like, "That was a cool guy. I was being awkward. Ugh, this is why I'm single."

After dropping the warm goodbye I've had those same women say something to me later in the night, somewhat apologetic for the way they acted before. If you try to drag the situation out and exit awkwardly that will never happen.

2. Everyone else is watching

As I mentioned earlier, other people in the area are often watching this interaction -- they know at the very least it can be pretty entertaining. So if you walk away awkwardly they'll all know what happened.

On the other hand, if you apply the warm goodbye with a smile and a toast, you'll now be giving everyone the impression that you're a friendly, social guy and you're leaving because those individuals aren't in the mood to talk at the moment. In fact, most observers won't know if you knew them already or not, giving the impression that you're a social guy who seems to know everyone. The women who do want to have a fun conversation with a cool guy will be more likely to shoot you some "I want you to talk to me" eye contact and be open to your company.

3. For you

Yes, the possibility of her rethinking her actions and of you gaining the admiration of everyone else in the area is nice, but the most important reason why you employ the warm goodbye is for you. As I mentioned, when you walk away awkwardly it confirms every insecurity you had in your head. Instead of telling yourself, *She didn't like me, I wasn't good enough*, telling them, "I've got to get back to my friends, you guys have a good one," allows you to feel in the moment what you now know in your head: it's not me, it's just the situation. She may be demonstrating that she's not in the mood to socialize right now for whatever reason, but the decision to end this interaction is mutual.

All you have to do is try it once to feel the powerful effect that this simple sentence can have on your psyche. Understanding something intellectually is one thing, but making it a reality though your conscious actions is another thing entirely. No one can ever reject you unless you let yourself be rejected. Take ownership of your life, and only interact with people you love interacting with.

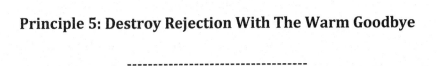

Principle 5: Destroy Rejection With The Warm Goodbye

SECTION TWO

How to Hold the Best Conversations

CHAPTER 6

The One Thing Every Great Conversationalist Does

Again and again, I hear two big problems involving the conversations guys care most about. First, "I always run out of things to say." Second, "I feel like I'm doing all of the talking and not getting much back in return." Raise your hand if you can relate to either of these -- ok, that's pretty much everyone in the universe.

I was once in the same place, too. But several years ago, I had an experience that illuminated and solved the issues frustrating most men I know.

I was on vacation in the beautiful city of Amsterdam, staying in one of the most popular hostels in town amid picturesque canals near the outskirts of the red light district. Hostels, by the way, are hands down the best place to meet new, interesting people to enjoy trips with -- especially when traveling alone. The very first evening confirmed this as I sat in a circle of my fourteen co-ed roommates, having some beers, trading stories, warming up for a fun first night on the town. Sitting directly to my right in the circle also happened to be a lovely blonde Romanian woman named Ana, with whom I had some chemistry. As the night wore on and we flirted more and more, she began leaning in closer and closer to me.

My vacation seemed to be off to a pretty great start, but as we all know, life can sometimes throw you a curveball.

That night, the curveball came in the form of three Norwegian guys, yelling and creating some commotion in the courtyard below. These guys were checking into the men's dorm just across the courtyard, and most of the women in our circle ran over to the window to see what was up. The ringleader of the group grabbed our window sill (on the 2nd floor) and pulled himself up into our room with the help of some of those enchanted women, and then stood in the center of our circle where he proceeded to hold court.

He was the proverbial "alpha male." He had a strong, commanding presence, held space well, and told stories and jokes, all the while having the group lingering on his every word. He perfectly embodied most people's stereotype of a master conversationalist. Not surprisingly, as I looked over to my right I saw Ana, not leaning toward me anymore but rather, toward him and giving him the look that told me her interests had shifted.

While I'm certainly not proud of this, I have to admit that my first reaction in the moment was jealousy. I mean I didn't necessarily want to be the center of attention, but I was afraid that everyone -- including Ana -- would forget about me in the wake of this new guy. Of course, my thoughts at the time weren't quite so introspective. They were more along the lines of "this guy's such a cocky asshole" and "how can these people be so enamored with his bs?" and "screw them, I'll be better off on this trip on my own."

I was a ball of negativity, unfairly dumping my own insecurities on everyone else. More than that, I was playing the victim: I felt hurt and initially didn't know what to do so I started blaming everyone and everything for my feelings. I was feeling sorry for myself the same way a guy who "doesn't

47

know what to say" simply shrugs his shoulders and feels sorry for himself because the conversation isn't going anywhere. While the situation may be different, closing up and pushing people away while making excuses and playing the victim is the same root, the same common rut.

Luckily, I became aware of what I was doing and those awful thoughts passed, only to be replaced by new ones. At least these new thoughts weren't all mopey and self-defeating like the last ones, but they were negative in their own way. They were: "Who does this guy think he's dealing with? I'm Nick Sparks -- I can be one hundred times more charismatic, funny, and charming than this clown. My stories would blow his out of the water. If I wanted to turn on my social power this guy wouldn't stand a chance."

This was my ego talking. I wanted to make it all about me -- "Look how great I am." I felt challenged, and my insecurity wanted to pull out the ruler and measure my manhood against this guy. While this rut looks different than the previous one, both have the same root -- my unacknowledged feelings, no sign of holding space. This is also one of my biggest ruts: I've always loved the spotlight, and have developed what most would call a fairly dynamic personality. This, however, has led to me sometimes making it "all about me" -- which is one of the surest ways to turn off everyone else.

Introverts I work with always think they need to be more like extroverts in order to be great conversationalists. In fact, extroverts often have the toughest time becoming great conversationalists because they're more deeply entrenched in this rut of making it about them and trying to win the other person over with their personality. Thus extroverts often feel like they're doing all the work and not getting much back in return.

I was very tempted to take this path, but for whatever reason I was fortunate enough to catch myself again. After holding space for those feelings and acknowledging them for what they were, the feelings started to dissipate a bit and my mind stopped racing. Then, by some small stroke of fortune, some very curious thoughts came into my mind: "Just because this guy is charismatic doesn't mean that everyone will forget about me. If that woman I had chemistry with is a better match for this guy then it's clearly not meant to be between us. Everyone else is enjoying themselves, I should too."

And so I stopped thinking and started listening. I held space for his stories and the emotions he imbued those stories with because he was in the moment while telling them. In truth, he was a pretty cool guy and it soon became clear why everyone else was having such a good time.

As I got more into the moment, giving him my full attention and vulnerably reacting to everything he was saying with my own genuine emotion, the most amazing thing happened. He started to react more strongly to me. As I gave him more genuine enthusiasm and interest he started giving me more of his energy and attention -- talking more directly to me than he was to the rest of the group.

As I reflected on this, I realized that I could relate. As someone who is prone to enjoying the spotlight, I knew how the most valuable thing I could receive was strong, genuine validation to what I was saying. From that perspective it came as no surprise that as I became his biggest fan, he became more and more interested in my interest.

He came closer and closer to me, almost turning what had been a group conversation into a two-man show. I realized that I was acting as a lightning rod for the energy in the room. My attention had drawn his momentum, and thereby that of the entire group, toward me. I realized then that **the most powerful social force in the universe isn't energy, it's space**.

At that moment I looked over to my right and saw Ana leaning back toward me, giving me those eyes that made my heart flutter.

This experience taught me very clearly what the best conversationalists already know: feeling down on yourself, being the victim, and using these excuses to keep from taking any action isn't going to get you anywhere. More importantly, what most people think of when they think of an amazing conversationalist -- being the uber-entertaining center of attention -- really doesn't matter either.

While being entertaining certainly doesn't hurt and can be fun, it can turn people off if it's coming from a place of insecurity. What really matters is how much space you leave for your own genuine emotion to come through and for others to express themselves. Would you rather dance for the entertainment of others or fully enjoy everything else around you? To put it another way, **would you rather be the jester or the king ... and would a woman prefer a jester or a king?**

The lesson I learned in Amsterdam when becoming the alpha's biggest fan turned everything around for me might sound familiar to you -- if you have read the classic self-help book, *How to Win Friends and Influence People* by Dale Carnegie. That lesson is basically the entire point of his book. Carnegie uses examples of remembering people's names, learning from dogs the importance of showing your happiness to see someone, and asking more questions about others rather than talking about himself at a wedding. Again and again he makes the point put incredibly succinctly in the old adage, "**It's better to be interested than interesting."**

If you're not actively enjoying others' company, they're going to be significantly less likely to let you know that they're enjoying your company, and less likely to want to talk to you more. Stop waiting for others to show that they like you and stop trying to figure out how to make that happen. If you hold space and let the others know that you're genuinely interested in them, then you'll have more success socially and professionally than you can imagine.

As for Ana, she and I had a wonderful rest of our trip together, and I still keep in touch with her today.

Principle 6: It's Better to Be Interested Than Interesting

CHAPTER 7

The Difference Between "He Was OK" and "He's Awesome"

Tony's biggest obstacle to meeting women wasn't his wheelchair. No, it was the way his perceived disadvantage made him believe he needed to overcompensate for it. He didn't believe women would find his natural personality attractive, so he needed to have clever things to say and do in order to entertain them.

Once again, he was trying to be interesting rather than interested. Even worse, when a woman was speaking, he'd barely be listening to her. Instead he'd be somewhere in his head trying to think of what he could say next to get her to like him. Her words would almost instantly become dry because she could tell that he was checked out of the conversation.

His self-confidence was getting attacked from both sides. On one hand, his attempts to always figure out the "right thing" to say subconsciously reinforced his core insecurity that he wasn't good enough as he was. On the other hand, the negative responses he got from women because he was barely listening to them reinforced his (mistaken) idea that women wouldn't be attracted to him no matter what he did.

What was especially tough for Tony was that he had invested a lot of time, hope, and energy -- as well as thousands of dollars -- in other coaches who reinforced the idea that he needed something interesting to say by feeding him clever lines or conversation topics. To invest yourself completely to improve at something -- yet to still fail -- sends a powerful message: "I'll never get this, my fears were right, women could never be attracted to someone like me."

While Tony's rut was deeper than most, it's very common for the clients I work with to try to always have the "right thing" to say to the women -- and yet this pressure to perform inevitably make them the most nervous. That should come as no surprise when we've been raised as a culture on movies and television shows wherein the hero seems to inevitably win the girl with some witty banter or clever line. This is then reinforced by the dating advice industry which was born in the same culture, 99% of which teaches lines to say and stories to tell in order to win a woman over. It's really no wonder then that one of women's most common complaints about guys is, "It doesn't even feel like he's listening to me, but rather just waiting for his turn to talk."

We've all heard how important "active listening" is, and we all make an attempt to at least appear as though we're listening. We make eye contact -- not in a vulnerable way, but rather "looking at her face because that's what you're supposed to do." So we gaze and smile and nod so that the other person won't notice how we are constantly jumping into our head to see if what they've said so far gives us anything to say next. Then we coast on autopilot with our "active listening" skills intact, keeping tabs on what we were going to say so we don't forget. We then offer a bland, "oh, cool" or "really, awesome," often cutting her off before she was finished -- because we weren't actually listening closely in the first place -- so we can quickly launch into the next piece of "brilliance" or clever repartée that we have to offer.

Of course the only person who lauds our communication skills at this point is ourselves. We thought we were being judged on having something witty to say to keep the conversation going, and we succeeded. Meanwhile, despite your nods and smiles, it was obvious to her that you were off somewhere else while she was saying something, everyone within earshot could tell that your, "oh, cool", was hollow, and there's not a single person on the planet that likes to be interrupted. Not even the cleverest of lines will make up for that.

However, when you're talking to a friend, you aren't focused on figuring out the next thing to say -- you just listen to them. You aren't trying to think of how you can extend the conversation and so the conversation just flows naturally. One of the most common things I hear from the guys I work with is that they're fine at making conversation most of the time, but with the women they're most attracted to, or anyone to whom they feel intimidated, they fall back into bad habits and things stall. The issue clearly isn't in your abilities, but rather in the way you're approaching the situation.

Just like my second impulse in the hostel in Amsterdam, we're trying to make it about ourselves ("Look at how funny, clever, and charming I can be!") Women don't want to be won over. Aside from making her wonder why you're trying so hard -- as if you need to desperately prove that you're good enough for her -- it makes her wonder why you think that whatever you have to say is more important than what she has to say.

Women, and men for that matter, don't want someone who tries to make himself the center of attention. Sure, we may be entertained by that person for a while but **ultimately we're most attracted to individuals who can make the moment between us the center of attention**. Women don't want you to hog the spotlight. Rather, they want to share it to create an intimate experience where times flies, and you just have the best time talking about nothing in particular. They don't want someone stressed over making everything perfect for her. What they want is someone enjoying their company just as much as they are enjoying yours.

The best model for this is a child listening to a good storyteller. That kid isn't trying to think of what he can say to make the storyteller laugh, and he isn't trying to think of the best reply to the story. His only goal is to enjoy the story. He's listening so intently that when the storyteller mentions the creaking at the end of the dark hallway the child begins to tremble. When the storyteller raises his arms and screams to announce the monster's surprising appearance, the child nearly jumps out of his seat. As any performer will tell you, you can't ask for a better audience than one who reacts emotionally like that, and there's no audience member who enjoys the show more.

I call this child-like form of listening "emotional listening" -- listening so completely that your first reaction is simply the expression of the emotion raised in the moment. When a woman is talking about her dog that died when she was a kid, you should look and feel as though your dog just died that second. When you find out that it's her friend's birthday, you should look and feel as though it's your birthday. When she tells you about a recent accomplishment, you should look and feel like you just accomplished the goal you're currently working to achieve.

Again, you can't fake it. If you start to creep into your head to think, "ok, she's telling a sad story, I should make my face look sad" she'll feel the disconnect, figure out your agenda, and immediately pull back herself. If you start to worry that your first reaction isn't the best one and instead try to craft the perfect response you'll find that her walls will fly up just as quickly.

Also, when you stop worrying about what to say, take that pressure off yourself, and just listen like a child, you'll find you are enjoying these interactions the way you always wanted to in the first place. That's really the biggest difference between a man who stands out and one who gets tossed back with the majority: are you in the moment, genuinely enjoying the company of the people around you or are you worried about what you should say? People feel great around the first person and nervous around the second.

Tony was equating listening and empathizing with dry, boring conversations. Instead, when you stop worrying and start making your top priority enjoying the other person's company you're helping to create the kind of interactions we never forget. Flirting happens when we allow ourselves to enjoy the sexual feelings that often arise when we hold space for them when interacting with others. Finding the other person boring? Most people are interesting two levels under the surface -- it's up to you to find out what that buried treasure is. If she's interested in sharing, feeling your genuine interest without agenda and the space you leave for both of your feelings will be what inspires her to open up.

As someone else is speaking, if you're listening attentively and holding space for whatever thoughts and emotions pop up your possible responses will be as numerous as the stars -- completely different from anyone else she'll ever meet. Because this reaction isn't twisted through some nervous thought process, but rather a genuine reaction to the moment, it will always be the most attractive thing you can say or do at the time.

I'll now list some of the most common reactions one has while emotionally listening so you have a clearer idea of what it looks like. As a point of reference, you can use any great conversation you've ever had.

EMPATHETIC EXPRESSION

The basis for emotional listening is the first feeling that comes up for you expressed through your body. Sometimes the situation can warrant a more colorful physical outburst, but the feeling expressed strongly through your eyes and expression on your face is most important.

Sometimes a quick verbal outburst accompanies this physical display of emotion as well. Saying, "Really?" when you're genuinely curious about something she said or "Oh my gosh" when she says something that genuinely surprises you will also convey your emotional reaction to whatever she said. Keep in mind the words by themselves are useless. They will definitely communicate that you're not listening to her if you say them without genuine emotion.

RELATING

Aside from our genuine emotion reflecting whatever she's saying, another response that we'll naturally experience when we're listening intently to someone else is that their words will remind us of an experience of our own. We already know about the attractiveness of vulnerability -- sharing the first memories that come up in that moment is another layer of that. If we don't share our experience, then the other person will become less and less comfortable sharing hers.

Just be sure to keep it brief and quickly bring the conversation back around to her. Getting too into detail about a particular topic that steers the conversation past intimacy and into minutiae is another common rut. Also, if you finish talking about yourself without any further expression of interest in her it leaves a validation-seeking vibe like "I hope you like what I just said." Instead, keep some version of "how about you?" ready before you either blab on for too long out of nervousness or wait for her to pass judgement.

ASKING DEEPER QUESTIONS

Not to be confused with asking more questions about a particular musician or travel destination (for example), which people can use to keep the conversation going without taking it to a more intimate level.

When you place yourself fully in someone else's shoes as they're speaking, you'll naturally see blanks they left out -- consciously or subconsciously. The feeling that typically arises in this moment is curiosity and simply by expressing that you'll always ask the "right question." If you're worried about asking the right question or the most interesting question you can possibly ask, then you'll always ask the wrong one.

As I mentioned, most people are interesting two levels beneath the surface, and so it's up to you to ask the right questions. What are you the most interested in knowing about them at that moment?

HUMOR

Human beings are absurd. The birth of consciousness and the ego gave rise to countless inconsistencies in how we speak and act. Worse, we take things seriously that aren't really very serious at all. If we didn't stop to laugh at ourselves and the reflection of our own absurdity in others we'd lose our minds.

When you're really listening to someone else and not just putting pressure on yourself to be funny, you'll notice and appreciate their jokes more as well as noticing more absurdities that they may have missed. I've never met anyone who wasn't funny as long as they weren't worried about trying to be funny. The trick is to include the other person in your joke. Let her see the amusement in your eyes and smile on your face as you highlight the absurdity so she can enjoy the joke with you instead of feeling like you're waiting for her to pass judgement on your attempt at humor. If something she said or did was silly or embarrassing, make sure you mention how "everyone does it" so that the absurdity is the butt of the joke instead of her.

***

This particular rut of Tony's may have been deeper than average, but we focused on moving past it, and he has probably made more progress than anyone I've ever worked with. The difference between your best conversations and your worst is how much you're worried about the outcome, about trying to make something happen. When you're not sabotaging yourself with this common rut, there's no magical formula to great interactions. They just happen.

When you express your genuine interest and hold space for both of your immediate emotional reactions, you are making your first priority -- your only agenda -- to enjoy connecting with someone. Not only will you be acting in the most genuinely attractive way possible but you'll also start enjoying your interactions so much more. When Tony focused on making this his top priority and dropped the need to win women over, he started enjoying his social life more. His big surprise came a week after his weekend with me when he held space with a woman he was having an awesome interaction with, and the feeling of mutual attraction just popped up -- without him having to "do anything" at all!

Principle 7: Enjoy Connecting with People & Go With Your First Instinct

----

CHAPTER 8

How to Easily Overcome Awkward Silences

You'll never find the right answer if you don't ask the right question.

Mateo not only struggled to start conversations, he also felt lost whenever a lull or "awkward silence" fell over any interactions he did manage to get going. He used the same excuse of "not knowing what to say" -- when in fact he just wasn't asking himself the right question.

Mateo was trying to be interesting, trying to fill the silences with whatever he thought she would like the most or what would be the cleverest thing he could say. Once again, it's better to be interested than interesting. Trying to impress her with the most interesting thing you can say will only make you look desperate and keep you awkwardly in your head instead of holding space and being present in the moment.

Instead of asking himself, "What can I say that will be interesting?" during a pause in conversation, the only question Mateo needed to answer was, "How can I show her I'm interested?" When you reframe the question in the correct light, the answer becomes much clearer.

Every conversation reaches a lull. A topic is introduced, you both chat back and forth for a number of minutes, relating and asking more personal questions, until you reach a point where no one has anything else to say on that conversational thread (this could take 2 minutes or an hour). At this point, someone has to introduce a new topic or "push the conversation forward" in order for it to continue.

You don't want to be the one to do this too often, otherwise the conversation turns into an interview. She'll start to contribute less and less while you feel as though you're doing all of the "work" to keep the interaction going.

At the same time, she shouldn't be pushing the conversation forward every time, lest she gets the impression that you're not interested in continuing to talk to her and that she's doing all of the work. In the end, this division of labor should be about 50/50, with each person taking turns pushing the conversation back and forth to each other, each equally showing that they want to keep talking with the other person.

Mateo thought he was losing conversations because he wasn't interesting enough -- but in reality the women he would speak to lost interest because they didn't think he was actually interested in them.

Questions such as "So where are you from?" are often spoken of disparagingly in the dating advice industry as something to avoid at all costs for being too boring and common, but they're the questions that most commonly come out of my mouth. There's a reason why we have these established go-to's -- they're a good way to get to know about someone you just met and show interest in the other person.

The problem comes in when guys just fire them off one after another, not because they're actually interested in getting to know her better, but because they're just trying to keep the conversation going as long as possible, hoping to hit on a topic she'll like. These questions aren't meant to set you apart -- the fact that you're actually interested in her responses and listening emotionally instead of trying to say the "right" thing will do that.

When I say, "Hey, how's it going?" it's not just something I say to get a conversation started, I actually want to know how they're doing in that moment. "What are you (guys) up to tonight (today)?" or "how are you enjoying the party?" will usually yield a half-assed response unless you actually care what they're doing. If you say, "where are you from?" as a way to elicit information that you can use to continue the conversation then she'll probably start writing you off as just another typical guy. If you genuinely enjoy talking about growing up in different parts of the world and want to get to know her better when you ask the same question, then she'll immediately feel that and know you're one of the guys that she rarely gets to meet.

It's also important not to rush to fill those first couple lulls either. This just sends the same message that you don't actually care about the conversation and are just trying to make it last longer or are desperately trying to meet some agenda. Instead, take a moment or three to emotionally reflect on what was just discussed and possibly share those feelings with her through eye contact before continuing the conversation. You'll probably be surprised as well, by the number of times she says something else when you give her the space to do so.

You don't approach conversations with friends with this mindset: "what do I say that they'll like talking about?" That's simply another rut your brain has developed to avoid being vulnerable with your feelings. Instead, when you feel your nerves rising in a conversation, simply be present with that excitement and express your genuine interest in the other person. When you're with your friend and you actually want to know what's going on in their life you might say, "so what's going on with you?" The words don't matter, all that matters is the feeling that you care. It's no different with a person you just met. It doesn't have to be fancy, it just has to be real.

While genuine interest is the catalyst for the interaction to continue, as noted above, it's still important not to turn the conversation into an interview. If she hasn't filled in the first or second lull I'll leave it to her to push the conversation forward the next time.

Letting the silence go can be incredibly nerve wracking when the other person intimidates you, and five seconds can feel like five minutes. You may be afraid the other person will get bored or feel awkward and not want to continue the conversation. In reality, while they'll certainly feel more tension in the silence, the worst thing you can do is show that it's too much for you by talking too much or retreating back onto your head. Instead, remind yourself that it's not your sole responsibility to make the conversation happen. Hold space for those nervous feelings and embrace them, and look at her, fully comfortable in the silence with a feeling of, "I can't think of anything to say. I still like talking with you. What are *we* going to do about this?" If she says, "what?" to break the tension you can always respond with some variation of those feelings. She'll most likely push the conversation forward if you've been in tune with her feelings up to this point whatsoever. If she doesn't, it happens, no big deal, and it's time to start thinking about employing the warm goodbye and ending the interaction.

This is precisely where Adam was going wrong. He was incredible at keeping a conversation going -- one of the best I'd ever seen. I'm pretty sure there was never a hint of silence in any of his conversations because he always had something to say to fill it in. He was a good listener and had no problem really being interested in other people. The problem was that Adam never allowed her to contribute to the conversation as well, often interrupting her before she was about to say something, and thus he was unwittingly sending the message, "I'm more interested in me than you."

Adam happens to be blind, and so he couldn't get the normal visual feedback that lets us know the other person is still 'with us'. Without that visual feedback he feared that if he wasn't constantly getting verbal feedback than she would lose interest in the conversation. I had Adam focus on slowing down -- holding space for his feelings instead of reacting to them out of fear with more words -- and not always pushing the conversation forward after the first or second time he's done that. He did so, and the first time the woman he was speaking to filled that silence and showed him that he didn't have to do all the work, it was a game-changer.

Just like Adam and Mateo, you will need to relax and take the pressure off yourself. Instead of stressing yourself out over having the right thing to say -- whether that fear drives you to silence or blabbing -- start asking yourself the right question: "How do I show her I'm interested in who she is and what she has to say?" You'll be surprised at how easy holding a conversation actually is.

Principle 8: Fill Silences With Genuine Interest And Allow Her to Share the Responsibility

----

CHAPTER 9

Your Secret Weapon for High-Voltage Interactions

It was the Friday night of my program, the second of three consecutive nights on the town, and David wasn't having the kinds of interactions that we both wanted him to have. Everyone seemed to have a good time in his conversations and he could get phone number without a problem, however his interactions lacked a certain charge and he felt dejected when they never returned his call or text.

Observing David, I quickly found the reason why his interactions lacked that charge. He was good at holding space, genuinely interested in the people with whom he was talking, and going with his first gut instinct in terms of what to say. That's why having solid conversations and getting phone numbers wasn't an issue. The problem was that during the interactions, he appeared and felt physically stiff and wasn't initiating any physical contact -- thus, while many women enjoyed his company, the interactions still felt a bit anxious.

When we're around people with whom we're comfortable, our bodies start to move together in a natural rhythm and we communicate through touch. Just like when you begin a conversation leaving that awkward half-step of distance, when you don't communicate with this natural physical rhythm and touch it says, "this is awkward." Holding space for our feelings and sharing them through eye contact are the two most powerful ways in which human beings communicate; after that, though, physical expression is next.

When we're feeling something strongly, whether it be empathy, happiness, or attraction, making physical contact with someone else will communicate those feelings more powerfully than words ever could. You may remember a time when a friend opened up to you about something tough in his life. Perhaps you couldn't think of the words to say, but you put your hand on his shoulder to let him know you empathized and that it would be alright.

In a 1976 study titled "Hands Touching Hands: Affective and Evaluative Effects of an Interpersonal Touch" (Fisher, Rytting, & Heslin), social scientists had a library clerk initiate a casual touch half the time when returning library cards to patrons. The results were that the individuals who were touched, even if they weren't aware of the touch, rated the clerk more positively than those who were not touched. Multiple studies since then have linked touch to the release of oxytocin, the chemical in the brain which increases the levels of trust and connection with another person.

Before even being aware of these scientific studies, from observing thousands of interactions I could tell that the amount of physical openness greatly determined the level of enjoyment and intimacy in the interaction. I began taking note of the most common physical expressions of intimacy in great interactions. Then I had my clients who had the most trouble with this use them as guidelines to allow their own physical expressions of intimacy to come forward when interacting with our female assistants in the classroom, and then later in the evening.

These are the platonic physical expressions I've distinguished from my own behavior in any great interaction I've had and through my professional experience. It's important to note that if you think about doing any of these things as a technique to increase intimacy you'll be in your head and the feeling of the interaction will be awkward. Instead, let these examples serve as a reminder to not hold back your own physical expression in the interactions that make you the most nervous.

PHYSICAL POLARITY

When two human beings have held space for and are present with the feelings in their body as they're connecting with each other, they'll both begin to notice a natural pull toward each other. When they inch closer their heart rates increase and the natural tension of the moment rises until they pull back and give each other more space to express the emotions they just felt before repeating this process over and over -- sometimes with more intense closeness, and sometimes with longer spaces. Just about every partner dance is based on this phenomenon (even ice dancing) and being great at it is the same as being "good" at physical expression in regular conversations -- it's all about listening and reacting to the feeling in your body at that moment.

I can glance at two people across a crowded room and tell you what their later activities will entail with alarming accuracy based on the intensity of their physical polarity and the vibe of the interaction, and I can also tell immediately when someone is sabotaging this natural process, either consciously or subconsciously. The two most common ways this is done subconsciously, when it comes to the physicality, are either being overly stiff and distant, thereby cutting off the connection, or by overthinking the closeness and moving in awkwardly and doing it too much, thereby weirding a woman out in a completely different way.

Physical polarity will look a little different in a book store or office place than a private party, but the natural rhythm that sets in when two people are in the moment enjoying each other's company is unmistakable. Become aware of ruts that may make you derail this process before either of you want the interaction to end, and let your body move in the way that will feel best for you in the moment.

HAND CHECKING

If one were to name the most basic form of platonic physical expression, it would be what I call the "hand check" -- simply extending your hand to touch a part of the other person's body, typically the shoulder, arm, or knee (if seated).

There's a good reason why it's the standard, as well. On one hand, it's very unobtrusive. If someone is uncomfortable with touch, slowly reaching your hand out toward their arm or shoulder will allow them to express their discomfort long before things would move to an awkward hug. On the other hand, as indicated in the example I used of you comforting your friend above, it can strongly communicate your feelings in a way that words cannot.

When you're comfortable with someone you often do this subconsciously to share some particular feeling more strongly. When you start paying attention to this natural inclination in your interactions, you'll begin to notice all the times you squash your desire to touch someone and sabotage the potential intimacy of the moment. The more attention you bring to it, the sooner you overcome that hesitation and start connecting on a deeper level.

ELBOW NUZZLING

I throw this one in because I want to make the point that natural physical expression is incredibly varied, and your own personality combined with your feelings in the moment will create some very eclectic expressions. Maybe you lean in to nudge someone playfully with your elbow, or maybe you playfully turn your back when you hear they went to Ohio State....

The point is that even aside from the emotional connection made through our eyes, human beings communicate a tremendous amount with our bodies. If you're inhibiting these expressions because you're tense or overthinking things, or if you try to force them, other people will not feel completely comfortable opening up to you and the connection will stagnate.

Once again, these aren't secret techniques that promise outlandish results -- they're what you naturally do with your friends and people with whom you're comfortable. When you don't do them you can come off as awkward and uncomfortable, which is usually the last kind of vibe you want to create between you and another human being. While you'll naturally feel more intimidated as you bring more consciousness to this rut and examine the fear behind it, the positive reactions you receive from people when you start communicating more fully will make this feel natural in no time.

***

That Saturday afternoon, along with the usual sexual communication, we had David put extra emphasis on getting comfortable with his physical expressions with our female assistants. His interactions that night all had that spark that was missing the night before, and he actually had to leave our Sunday session a little early to sneak in a last minute date before his flight.

For me though, my favorite part happened as I observed David Saturday night. When he stopped holding back his physical expression out of nervousness, you could see how much more he was opening up and enjoying himself in the moment throughout his entire evening. That enjoyment was what attracted everyone to David that night -- the rhythm they moved with and the way they touched each other was simply a byproduct.

Principle 9: Let Your Body Go & Unlock the Full Potential of Your Interactions

----

SECTION THREE

How to Get Sexual Like a Man

CHAPTER 10

Why You Must Get Sexual

It's rare for me to work with a guy who is comfortable expressing his sexuality. The main sexual education we received growing up was "wear a condom," yet it was never actually explained how one gets to the point where the condom is applied. We were left to figure this out on our own. It's rare to flip through a magazine or turn on the TV without being bombarded by erotic images that make us feel very advanced sexually, but when it comes to acting sexually those images leave us with more questions than answers. We're taught how to look sexy, but I've worked with male models who will tell you that will only get you so far.

Of course we had the "help" of movies and television, which basically taught us that after the socially-awkward guy saves the world the beautiful woman looks at him and says, "So when are you going to ask me out on a date?" -- or some variation. The guy then laughs nervously and she kisses him. This is the fantasy of socially-awkward film writers, not of most women who want a man who's not afraid to express his desire confidently.

When the end of the world isn't setting up the romance, movies will give us scenarios where two people who are just attracted for no apparent reason go at it. But we're never really taught the mechanism by which this all happens.

Growing up with this limited knowledge, many guys struggle with the idea of exactly when or how they're supposed to express their sexual feelings. Some worry that they'll "mess up" an interaction that's going well if they express their sexual desire too soon. They're afraid that if they attempt to get sexual they'll be labeled as "creepy."

These men wait for the "perfect moment," which ends up never coming. They will end up dating a woman those rare times when she makes it easy for him and initially displays her desire aggressively, but they'll never feel like they're with a woman because they chose her and will often feel like they're settling, not necessarily with the woman but with themselves because they know they have yet to overcome the fear of expressing their sexuality.

Maybe they try being blindly aggressive to reverse this trend and numb themselves to their fear but they still turn off more women than they seem to turn on and the few that hook up with them never to return their texts. Despite the uptick in sexual activity, it's a double blow to the confidence. With the main options for further education being Maxim and the quagmire of misinformation that is the internet, it's no wonder so many men resign themselves to being the "nice" guy who quietly feels undesirable.

The great thing is, despite our depressingly poor education on sexual communication, it's hardwired into our DNA, and because of this we've all experienced sexual interactions in our lives. Even if you've never been physically intimate with a woman, you've still had at least one interaction that has taken on a more sexual tone, where your heart started to beat faster and the tension in the conversation belied the mundane content of your words ... most likely a conversation where you were "on" or she started flirting first.

The point is, you've got the equipment to do this and you've already used it to some extent. The only challenge is understanding how it works so you can stop your ruts from interrupting the magic and live the kind of sexual life you were meant to.

The story told by our society in movies and TV on how the dance of attraction works, and the story retold by most dating advice, is that the man sees a woman and is attracted by her beauty, he showcases his value in some way in order to attract her, she becomes turned on by this display of value and shows her interest, and he then takes his "prize." This story -- which has its roots in a long-ago era in which the virgin in the ivory tower was the trophy to be won by the brave knight (thereby becoming his property) -- not only sets up an objectifying relationship between men and women but also does a poor job of educating us on how sexual attraction naturally works. This story leaves a lot of men feeling like the signals he's getting from a woman aren't strong enough for him to make a move (since he hasn't "won" her yet), and that he must still do something else before he's allowed to communicate his sexuality, lest he be deemed creepy. This lesson is also one of the reasons why extroverts never get as much back in return as they were expecting after "putting on a show" to win the affection of a crowd.

The way human attraction actually works when we remove this Hollywood fantasy is that human beings will sometimes feel "turned on" or aroused around other individuals for a multitude of reasons, social and biological. A study done by Swiss biologist Claus Wedekind in 1995, commonly referred to as the "sweaty t-shirt study," showed that women who smelled a series of sweaty tee shirts worn by various men were more physiologically turned on after smelling certain shirts than others. Sometimes a woman finds me attractive, sometimes I'm not her type.

Sometimes this natural attraction will pop up when two people interact -- when they're around each other, look each other in the eye, and especially when they open up more to one another. The interaction will appear on the surface like any other great interaction you've had, but the feeling will be different since it's imbued with that natural chemistry. Again, for reference, think of any great flirtatious interactions you've ever had.

Aside from the conscious reason to stop for whatever reason, the main thing that interrupts this process is our ruts. One of us jumps into our head, worries about saying the right thing or not messing it up. We start talking too much, pull away awkwardly, wonder when she's going to give us the big signal that we've won her over, wonder what else we can do to win her, or make a desperate move borne out of fear of loss. Whenever one of your ruts -- or your conscious decision to halt things -- interrupts this process she'll usually feel that and pull back immediately.

One of the main reasons we retreat into our ruts in an interaction with a woman we're attracted to -- instead of trusting our feelings -- is that we're not getting that aggressive response from the woman that we were taught to expect by our Hollywood fairy tales. We don't get that strong showing of desire, so we lock away any expression of desire we might have to prevent feeling rejected. The woman often then assumes we're not attracted to her, or uncomfortable with our sexuality, and quickly dismisses any feelings of attraction she might have felt.

Since you're usually not going to get those over-the-top signals, you have to learn to read and react to the feelings of the moment. Until you get better at doing so, here are some signals you can use as guidelines to know when it's ok to let your own expressions of desire flow worry-free:

EYE CONTACT

Not that "looking at someone's face" eye contact, but rather what I describe in Chapter 1. Revealing your feelings through your eyes is incredibly vulnerable. If she's trusting you with her feelings in that way you can take it as a pretty strong signal to let nature continue to flow.

FILLING IN THE SILENCES

When you leave those silences in an interaction does she fill them? I usually appreciate when she does because it's a sign that she doesn't want the interaction to end. This signal could mean that she's interested in talking with you more romantically or platonically -- only the feelings will know for sure. At the very least though, when she fills in that silence you can relax and continue to enjoy the conversation.

REAL EMOTION

Is the smile on her face a polite one, or is it radiating real emotion? When she speaks, is she fully present with her words, or does she seem off in her head somewhere? This is another signal that also applies to friendship (understandable why we get confused) but again, at the very least it means you have the green light to relax and allow things to continue forward. Is she off in her head somewhere? You already feel the distance, listen to it and don't wall yourself off or disconnectedly push forward.

HIPS DON'T LIE

You can place this signal right up there with vulnerable eye contact in terms of intensity of intimacy. Human beings will naturally open their hips toward what they're most attracted to at that moment. If you and a woman are completely facing each other while you're interacting (you'd naturally mirror each other if you're not in your head worried about body language) then you've either got a new best friend on your hands or an intense sexual connection.

***

Think back to all of the times when you received at least two of these signals from a woman while feeling that natural attraction in your body and you didn't allow your sexual interest to be expressed. Maybe you weren't sure how or maybe you were waiting for her to give you the most obvious signal ever based on something you did. In many of those situations she was trying to say, "I like you," and you replied, "Sorry, not interested." Think of how many times you were frustrated that things didn't work out when it was in fact you who rejected her because you were afraid to let your feelings be felt.

Again, these signals can also just mean that she just wants to be friends. If you express your desire in the ways I describe in the following chapters and she doesn't feel the same way, don't take it personally -- she just didn't like the smell of your sweat. And don't keep trying to be sexual in order to try to create a moment that's not naturally being created: that's how you come off as creepy. Instead, just continue to enjoy this other human being's company. It can be difficult not to take it personally when you're starved for any sort of sexual intimacy. But once you stop holding your sexual feelings back and start enjoying all of the sexually charged interactions you were meant to it will be much easier to ignore the times there isn't any chemistry, rather than letting them reinforce the idea you're undesirable.

It's an imperfect system, and in the future I hope that men will get better at reading the feelings of the moment and communicating with their own. I also hope that women will become more understanding of the language men were taught to communicate in and get more comfortable expressing their desire overtly without fear of being called a "slut." Until then, though, we have to do our best to do our part -- to listen to our feelings and express them genuinely because we felt them, not because she made some grand gesture of her own.

Principle 10: Instead of Trying to Win Her Over, Confidently Express Your Feelings

----

CHAPTER 11

How to Flirt Like a Pro

Eric was a good-looking guy by all accounts. He was a great listener, started going with his first gut response instead of overthinking things, and began relaxing his body after our first night working together. Thus, he got some pretty terrific responses. Women were lighting up in conversations with him and for a moment I had to wonder why he needed my help.

Then it became clear. After getting some of the best responses I'd ever seen on both Thursday and Friday nights, Eric's interactions would start to fizzle in five to ten minutes. When he did get a woman's number after a seemingly awesome conversation, she would often not respond to his texts. At this point it wasn't surprising to hear that he was madly attracted to a woman back at home, Kaitlin, who only saw him as a friend, laughing awkwardly whenever he tried to express his romantic feelings. After reading the previous chapter (and the title of this one), you should already have a good idea of where Eric was going wrong.

Eric wasn't getting sexual. When sexual feelings naturally arose in an interaction he became uncomfortable, muffled them, and kept all of his communication strictly platonic -- creating an awkward vibe. Maybe sexual communication was repressed in his upbringing. Maybe he was taught to wait for some big signal from a woman that usually doesn't happen. Maybe he just never learned how -- or possibly all three. And so even after meeting a woman who was very much attracted to him initially, she would eventually move on to find a guy that wasn't afraid to show her that he was attracted to her.

Kaitlin may have found Eric attractive initially, but after he effectively demonstrated that he wasn't a sexual being (despite making some jokes on the subject) there really wasn't a chance for those feelings to continue.

"Sexy Saturday" of the program, the day we practice sexual communication with our female assistants, was really a revelation for Eric. After explaining why these interactions would flail (as discussed in the previous chapter) I explained that sexual communication started and ended with the natural sexual energy that you feel in that specific moment.

You may have heard the expression, "It's not what you say, it's how you say it." If you've ever been angry or irritated about something, it doesn't matter what you say to someone else, they're going to feel the fact that you're angry or irritated. Similarly, if you say, "I hate you," but you do it affectionately in the same way one would say, "I love you," then no one is actually going to believe that you hate them.

Flirting is the same way. If you try to speak sexually or get more physical but you're not actually feeling turned on inside -- either because you're because you're in your head or because you've diffused them through other nervous habits -- then she won't feel that you're actually attracted to her. Your words and actions will feel awkward and phony, and she'll most likely brush them off or act like you're joking.

Close your eyes, picture a woman that really turns you on. Imagine her scantily clad or wearing nothing at all and doing every sexual thing that your heart could ever desire, fulfilling your every fantasy, your bodies pressed against one another in whatever way you want. Seriously, take a moment to close your eyes and imagine this.

Do you feel that swelling of energy in your chest (and other parts of your body)? Do you feel that natural, God-given tingling sensation resonating from the top of your head to the tip of your toe? Some people call it being turned on, while others call it horniness. I simply call it sexual energy.

When that feeling arises in an interaction with a woman -- if things are going to move forward romantically -- she has to feel that desire burning through you, resonating in your chest and communicated through your entire body. If you're feeling that energy and communicating it while listening to her feelings, then your actions will always be the "right" ones. If you're disconnected from that sexual energy, or you're in your head worried about messing things up, breaking eye contact or overdoing it out of desperation -- then she'll interpret the tension as awkward more than sexual or feel like you're not really into her. You can't think your way out of this bag. You have to trust your feelings.

Guys often ask me how they can lower their anxiety before talking to women to make things easier. I always say that you don't want to lower your level of energy, as this is what creates the spark or sexual tension in the interaction. Instead, you have to learn how to become comfortable with that energy so that you don't diffuse it in a number of nervous habits and excuses or other sabotaging thought patterns. You have to embrace that energy and learn how to ride the dragon. Human beings are attracted to individuals who can carry large amounts of tension or sexual energy while remaining calm. They want a man who won't flinch as she unleashes all of her sexual energy, who she can trust to hold the energy for both of them as she lets herself go. If you're showing that you can't handle this initial tension then she won't feel comfortable turning up the heat even further with you.

As you work on holding rising levels of sexual tension in your body without becoming anxious, these feelings will naturally be communicated through your body. We'll be describing how this happens through your touch and your words in the next two chapters. But the most important way your sexual feelings express themselves is through the feelings shared by both people in an interaction -- otherwise known as the vibe.

The most powerful way your desire is communicated in the moment it arises is through your body. As I mentioned, when someone is feeling something in their body whoever's around will feel it as well. As you become comfortable feeling more sexual energy in your body, your eyes and facial expression will reflect that energy, becoming more seductive. At the same time your voice will lower ever so slightly and take on a more seductive tone. Note that if you're trying to look or sound sexy, your expression will be as awkward as a fake smile. The expression has to be the one that naturally arises from the sexual energy of the moment.

If you want an excellent example of communicating with a sexual vibe, I recommend watching the television show Californication. The show revolves around the character Hank Moody, played by actor David Duchovny, who sabotages his life through countless sexual trysts. While television shows have to make the dialogue more "punchy" for ratings, you'll notice that the main driver behind Moody's trysts is the fact that he communicates with everyone in that show, men and women (with the exception of his daughter) with the most overt sexual tone you can imagine. The women he's interacting with feel this sexual energy and respond with flirtation of their own. At that point all Hank has to do is push things forward with an even more overt sexual vibe and the words and actions I describe in the following chapters.

Other than allowing her to contribute equally to the conversation, this is the area where not rushing to fill in silences is most important. Sexuality can't exist without silence, and although filling in this silence is one of the most common ways we diffuse the tension, you must avoid this rut if the natural sexual feelings of an interaction are to flourish.

The vibe is, by far, the most important factor in sexual communication. If you physically express your attraction but she can't feel that it's real, then she'll often brush off your advances unless she's just looking for a quick physical connection herself. If you verbally express your attraction but are in your head, thinking about what you should or shouldn't do, instead of feeling turned on, then she'll laugh your words off and tell you to stop kidding around, or she'll tell you you're sweet but she doesn't *feel* the same way. **She has to feel the sexual desire of the moment communicated through you without distraction in order to believe that your other advances are genuine.**

Communicating in a sexual vibe is often all you need. Maybe you're at a dinner party and you can tell two people are attracted to each other just by watching the way they communicate. Individuals who don't understand sexual energy wonder what happened. They ask, "What did he do to trigger that attraction?" and feel frustrated that they're not having those kinds of interactions with women. People who are aware of how sexual energy is communicated know exactly what's going on in this situation, -- often before the two people who are communicating sexually know it themselves -- and they just smile. They know that the two had some natural chemistry and that they weren't afraid to express their feelings for one another in the only way that matters. It's a beautiful thing.

In that Saturday afternoon classroom session, I'll think of something that turns me on and then talk about what the guys ate for breakfast with a sexual vibe. While the effect won't be as genuine as if I'm interacting with a woman with genuine sexual attraction present, the point I'm trying to convey to the guys is that the specific content of your conversation doesn't matter. Flirting often happens amid the most boring of subject topics. This is because **true sexuality isn't communicated via the content of your words; it's communicated in the subtext.**

Flirting, a concept which confuses most people who attempt to define it, is simply communicating with a sexual vibe. At its most basic level, it's acknowledging the natural attraction between two individuals and having fun with it. At a restaurant, you can flirt with a waitress without any sort of goal other than making each other's day a bit more enjoyable. Maybe one or both of you will prefer to leave it at that, or maybe you'll both be interested in more and will continue a conversation with that more personal tone before a number is exchanged.

You can toss around the slightest bit of sexual tone in your workplace. Many men and women use this -- and the boost in perceived confidence and charisma that comes with it -- as a means of having more fun and more enjoyable interactions with other office mates who also enjoy a little flirting. **Expressing your sexuality isn't about doing something extra, it's about being comfortable with all of yourself.** This perceived boost in confidence and charisma also gives them a slight edge to get ahead more quickly.

It's also important to note once again that you shouldn't be trying to do anything. Trying to feel sexual isn't holding space -

- holding space is remaining as quiet on the inside as possible and feeling the natural feelings that come up. When you try to force sexual feelings on the moment in order to achieve a desired outcome it will just feel desperate and manipulative. When you enjoy whatever comes up without agenda, due to the nature of human beings, those feelings will often be sexual.

If you only communicate sexually around the women to whom you're most attracted, you'll do so poorly. Sexual communication should be a natural part of all communication between consenting adults. As you practice holding space in all of your interactions and become more comfortable with your sexual energy, you'll notice slight sexual feelings popping up when you'd least expect them to. Sexual energy isn't exclusively about wanting to get more physical with someone. At its most basic level it's simply acknowledging, "this interesting thing often happens when two human bodies are around each other -- let's have fun with it for its own sake." Flirt with older women to remind them of their femininity, which is too often discarded by our society because it doesn't help us advance our personal agenda. Make them feel beautiful and not only will you enjoy your life more, bring more joy to others' lives, and become a better flirt, but don't be surprised when they want to introduce you to their daughter or granddaughter. If someone's not in the mood to flirt? It's easy to pull back to the platonic tone that you're more than comfortable with, no harm, no foul. The more you flirt with everyone, though, and make all women feel beautiful without agenda, the more the feminine population will reward you.

No matter what made you hold back from doing these things in the past, today is as good a day as any to start flirting. The best part is that when you start feeling and communicating just a little bit of sexual energy the moment it pops up, you'll notice an immediate positive difference in the responses you receive. Just remember that it's not about looking or sounding a certain way, but rather, *it simply comes from holding space for the feelings of the moment and reacting to them.*

By now you can probably guess what happened with Eric. Saturday night his mind was blown by just how many women were attracted to him when he wasn't afraid to express his sexuality. He headed home full of confidence, finally comfortable with all of himself, and now I have a letter from Kaitlin thanking me for bringing out the perfect boyfriend that was right under her nose.

Principle 11: Flirt with Everyone by Expressing Your Sexuality with Your Whole Body

----

CHAPTER 12

From Friend to Lover: How to Get Physical

When it comes to initiating a more intimate physical connection, men often face the same fear that they did when it came to expressing their sexual feelings in the first place -- making the move too soon and being rejected. They can put it off, again waiting for the "perfect moment" (where she makes it easy for him, movie style) which never comes, leaving the woman with the impression that he was interested in nothing more than a good flirt.

Fortunately for us, if you're present with the feelings of the moment and letting physical polarity run its natural course as I describe in Chapter 9, then physical sexual communication will naturally occur.

When two people are sexually attracted to each other, feeling that desire in their bodies and expressing it through flirting, both will naturally feel their bodies drawn toward each other much more aggressively than when only platonic feelings are present. When sexual attraction is present in the moment, every time you touch will feel amazing for both parties -- qualitatively different than the pleasant feeling a platonic touch brings. It feels like your body is wrapped in a blanket of tingly awesomeness when you can feel her next to you in that moment, and to be just a half-inch away from her feels incredibly sexy, building the tension before you touch again.

Physical communication of sexuality is simply the expression of your body's natural, God-given desire to be on each other. It's simply allowing yourself to convey that natural desire and begin feeling your body against hers in a way that feels great for both of you. The initial "steps" toward this form of sexual communication are no more intrusive than platonic physical polarity -- only the feeling will be different -- and thus you have plenty of time to "take the hint" if she doesn't feel the same way and prevent any grand rejection.

In the rest of this chapter I will give examples of the ways that human beings typically express their sexual desire physically. Just as with everything else in this book, if you try to consciously do any of these things as a 'move' then your actions will reek of awkwardness and agenda and be more likely to make her uncomfortable. Instead, your only jobs are, first, to not get in the way when your natural desire to get close to her takes over, and, second, to be present with her to make sure she's with you every step of the way.

PHYSICAL POLARITY 2.0

Again, when the vibe becomes sexual the usual level of physical polarity that occurs when the feelings are only platonic becomes much more intense. The feeling will certainly be different, and that will propel the two bodies to get even closer. While physical polarity must always involve moving closer, and then further away, the average distance between two people who are sexually attracted to each other will shrink more aggressively as these revolutions transpire.

When you're connecting with someone, you'll naturally move closer to them as you speak. The more you're turned on by that person in the moment, the closer you'll want to get. It'll become less about communicating whatever words you want to say and more about communicating that when you get closer to her it feels amazing.

When you lean in to say something, more and more of your bodies will make contact, from your shoulders to your hips. You'll catch a whiff of her scent and that draws you even closer to her ear and neckline as you speak. The feeling of your breath on the back of her neck and your lips barely grazing her ear sends shivers down her spine. You'll still lean back to give each other space to process the emotional intimacy you just shared, but your hips will linger closer and closer to each other as if they can't bear to be parted -- hence the expression, "attached at the hip."

Anyone who has ever said, "I don't like that place, it's too loud" about a bar or club -- if

they're interested in sexual connection -- obviously doesn't understand the way this natural phenomenon works. If you've ever found yourself "hooking-up" with someone after a night of too many drinks and aren't really sure how it happened, I can clear that up for you:

You saw someone with whom you had strong sexual chemistry. The loud music forced you to get closer to talk to them and jumpstarted the physical polarity. The alcohol kept you out of your head and stopped your natural ruts from sabotaging the process, as well as keeping any perfectly plausible reasons to slow things down from entering your mind, and you quickly became attached at the hip. The process of physical polarity then continues unabated until the next morning when our heads come back into play.

Again, if you try to do any of this as a strategy to turn her on or create sexual intimacy, you won't be holding space for the incredible feelings of the moment and she'll usually start to feel uncomfortable (unless she simply wants to get laid). Plus, it's much more fun for you when you can just surrender to the feelings of the moment and enjoy the ride.

HAND HOLDING

Despite being considered a more juvenile means of expressing physical attraction, holding hands is sexy -- it's not surprising that Lennon and McCartney wrote a song about it. There are a lot of nerve endings in our hands. When two people are sexually attracted to each other their hands will almost be drawn toward each other like magnets, and when they make contact you'll feel an explosion of warm gooey pleasure (if you're present with the feelings of the moment). It's almost as if our bodies want to talk to each other and the simplest way they can do that is through our hands.

A little afraid to go straight in for the hand hold? That's okay. When you're leaning in during one of the natural cycles of physical polarity it's not uncommon for your hand to brush against hers. When this happens, is her reaction one of comfort or discomfort? If you're continuing to get a connected vibe from her you can take that as a sign to let the natural process continue and allow those hands to talk.

TAKING HER HIPS

Don't ask me why, but there's something insanely sexy about putting your hands on or around a woman's hips. When you're turned on, you'll usually feel an intense desire to wrap your hands firmly around her hips and pull her as tightly toward you as possible.

I said that everything in this book applied to everyone no matter whom you were attracted to --well this may be the one exception. Whoever prefers the more dominant role in that moment will typically desire to do the hip taking, while the person who prefers the more submissive role in that moment will typically desire to have her (or his) hips taken.

The initial phases of this process will involve lightly running your hand along her hips, or flirting with them a bit. If she shows pleasure at this flirtation you have the green light to allow this natural process to continue gradually, taking her hips in one, and then both hands with greater intensity, culminating in pulling her toward you.

The more slowly this process develops the better. If she extends her hips toward you though, moving them in a sexy rhythm, you should give in to your desire to reach out for them -- if you're holding space for your feelings there's typically nothing you'll want more -- even if she then pulls back coyly to allow the dance to continue.

THE KISS

The problem most guys face when thinking of going for the kiss is that they try to cover a large distance with an awkward lunge. If you're not interrupting the natural flow of physical polarity 2.0 though, you can see that you should never have to worry about covering all that distance at once. When your bodies are getting closer, your hands holding each others' and running up and down her hips as they press more tightly against yours, your lips grazing against her cheek before looking deeply into her eyes, licking respective lips as you glance at them, your faces mere inches apart ... at this point it's nearly impossible to stop a kiss from happening.

***

If you're in your head, worried about getting physical the right way or trying to turn her on, then your actions will feel either stiff or forced and your touch will feel awkward. Instead, if you touch her in the way the feels best for you in that moment, then it will be the touch that will most likely feel best for her as well. You'll still have to pay attention to her physical and emotional response, but if you've been allowing the tension to build slowly and staying present with the shared feelings of the moment then nine times out of ten she'll be enjoying that touch just as much as you are.

If, for whatever reason, either one of you is uncomfortable proceeding to deeper levels of physical intimacy in that moment, then it's time to place a momentary hold on allowing the physical polarity to intensify and instead enjoy swimming around in whatever level of intimacy you're both comfortable with. If either of you becomes frustrated when the other expresses his or her boundaries, it's typically a sign that you had some agenda or preconceived notions about the other person that didn't take his or her feelings into account. In these instances the other person will rightfully feel creeped out and will usually pull away even more. If, on the other hand, both people are simply enjoying the natural attraction between them at a level they're both comfortable with showing that they both care about the other person's feelings, then it becomes increasingly difficult to stop the natural process of physical polarity from continuing.

There are some incredibly good reasons to stop things from getting more physical though, even if nature is telling you otherwise: if either of you are in an exclusive relationship, if it would hurt a friend, if she's giving you all of these signals and advancing things physically but she's not emotionally present. I could dedicate an entire chapter to this topic alone.

Even if you stop the physical dance from continuing, however, you should still hold space for the feelings of the moment and acknowledge them. In one of the above situations where it's best not to take things further, a polite smile of appreciation for the pleasant feelings will do just fine. If you try to repress those feelings your interactions will be laced with the awkwardness of your shame, and you're far more likely to "act out" in ways that damage your relationships.

This physical dance, from beginning to end to new beginning, is one of the most pleasurable experiences known to humanity. Exploring our relationship to it consciously and listening to the feelings that arise will, for many people, feel like exploring it for the first time. Embark fearlessly, and remember that as with many of life's journeys, it's not about getting to the destination, it's about enjoying the ride.

Principle 12: Sex Happens, Not When You Make It Happen, but When You Let It Happen

----

CHAPTER 13

How to Turn Up the Heat With Your Words

Speaking sexually often raises the same fears in men as initiating physical contact and flirting; they're afraid to come across as creepy. Often they've watched other men say things to women that they could only dream about, while any attempt of their own to turn the conversation in a more sexual direction is only met with awkward looks or uncomfortable laughter.

The concept of speaking sexually may be confusing to a lot of people who equate flirting with saying explicitly sexual things. As I discussed in Chapter 11 though, you can talk about breakfast and still flirt -- it's all about the vibe. Explicit sexual communication, on the other hand, is any verbal communication that directly expresses the sexual feelings you're experiencing in that moment. Basically, it's anything that verbally says, "I desire you."

Many guys make the mistake of thinking about verbally communicating their sexuality in terms of how they can turn on a woman with their words -- saying something that will get the sexual juices flowing. This also harkens back to the "winning her over" mindset that's one of the biggest turnoffs for women. Your goal shouldn't be to try to turn her on, but to express your feelings, which in this case are that she's turning you on. Just like with everything else in this section, your words must stem from the feeling of your sexual energy as you say them, otherwise they'll lack power and authenticity.

With that in mind, here are the most common ways that one expresses his desire verbally. As with the touching, this isn't a playbook or step-by-step instruction. This is what typically happens when you verbally react to the sexual energy of the moment.

COMPLIMENTS

The oldest form of expressing your attraction verbally (other than some sexual grunts), compliments have recently gotten a bad rap in the world of dating advice. I've heard that you shouldn't compliment women because they're so used to being bombarded by compliments from men that they've grown tired of them and you'll just be considered another boring guy if you do it.

True, plenty of guys have gotten less than positive responses when attempting to give a compliment, and these experiences have given some credence to the above interpretation of those experiences. But the reason why our compliments can receive mixed reactions is that we've abused them to the point of women being unable to trust us when we give them.

By "abused," I mean that men have misused compliments; instead of expressing genuine appreciation over something she did, many men use compliments to try to get a positive reaction out of a woman if he's not getting one already. In this way, the compliment isn't an honest one, but one whose purpose is to attempt to manipulate her emotions to give him his desired response. It's no different than when a salesman gives you an obviously fake compliment that turns you off from buying what he's selling. Is it any wonder that these phony compliments will turn a woman off after she's fallen for them once or twice in her life?

Instead, if a compliment reflects genuine feelings of appreciation -- when she's done something to inspire that appreciation -- then she will most likely react to it by lighting up like a Christmas tree. Maybe she'll even blush a little. For example, if she smiles politely but disingenuously and you say, "You have a nice smile," then it's kind of BS, and she probably won't respond very well. If, on the other hand, she smiles brightly and genuinely and you say, "I love your smile, it makes me happy," then it's a genuine compliment brought on by the real emotion you're feeling, and without any other agenda. As a result, she'll probably blush and smile even more adorably than before.

If you calmly say, "That's awesome," before launching into whatever you wanted to say next, she won't actually believe that you thought what she said was awesome. If you hold space for a few moments before saying, "I think that's really cool" -- while genuinely feeling impressed and looking her in the eye while conveying that feeling -- then she will smile and want to talk even more about whatever you're genuinely interested in.

GETTING A PHONE NUMBER

Guys often abuse getting a woman's phone number as well. They treat it as a trophy, trying to rack up as many numbers as possible as a way to gauge how well they're doing with women, and then wonder why most of those numbers never turn into dates.

Getting a phone number shouldn't be a goal or a trophy, it's merely a way of telling a woman that you're interested in spending more time getting to know her. If she's not getting that vibe from you, it doesn't matter if she gives you her number or not, she probably won't want to talk to you again.

On the flip side, too many guys hesitate to ask for her number after a fantastic conversation, once again waiting for some grand signal that she's interested instead of courageously expressing their feelings. Meanwhile, the woman just assumes that he's not that interested in her and doesn't want to see her again. Again, the world is changing and more and more women are initiating the number exchange, but we're still in a transitional period and many women will still wait for a guy to make the first move.

If you're talking to a woman, and there's an awkward pause, and then she says she needs to get going, and then another awkward pause, and then an awkward goodbye, many guys will interpret this as "Well, it got awkward, so she lost interest and shot me down." But from the woman's point of view it often went more like so: "He didn't ask for my number, so he wasn't that into me." When she says she has to get going it often really means, "Do you want my number or not dude?" If you're talking to two women and the one you've been communicating with more platonically excuses herself for any reason that leaves you alone with her friend with whom you've had more sexual chemistry, they're both expecting you to take her friend's number if you're interested in seeing her again.

To illustrate this point, one time I was eating in Whole Foods and got to talking with a lovely brunette who worked at the YMCA downstairs. I was in an exclusive relationship at this point and wasn't interested in anything more than conversation, but we were having a very nice conversation, and I could feel a tiny bit of attraction brewing between us. As

I was getting ready to leave, I could feel that moment arrive when I either ask for the number or not. I could feel her curious disappointment as I said goodbye without going for it. Because I didn't want her running back to Cosmo to try to figure out what she did wrong, I went back to the table after throwing out my trash and let her know that I didn't get her number because I was in a relationship but otherwise would have. She smiled and thanked me and said she was wondering if that was the case, but she couldn't be sure.

On one hand, going for a number says a lot. I've had women unwilling to kiss me because they thought I was just interested in a one night stand, but after taking their phone number because I really was interested in seeing them again things heated up physically in a hurry.

On the other hand, it's never over-the-top or inappropriate. If you're talking to a woman during the daytime, or maybe to a waitress at a restaurant where it's inappropriate to get closer physically -- when you're not sure if she likes you or is just flirting for fun or working for tips -- then you can just go for the number. As long as you ask for the number while feeling and communicating your sexual desire then her response will let you know immediately how she feels about you. If she's interested, everybody wins, if not then no harm no foul. I've gotten plenty of free drinks from bartenders after previously asking for their number, because they feel flattered and can't fault me for asking if they've been flirting with me. The best part though is that you'll never be left wondering what could have been.

When it comes to the phone number, your job is to make the awkward exchange happen as smoothly as possible. To accomplish this, I simply say some variation of, "I like talking to you, we should do it again," or "This is fun, I'd love to see you again" -- whatever I'm feeling in the moment. You're basically just verbalizing what the phone number implies, which is, "I want to see you again." As I'm saying this I'm already reaching for my phone, because if she agrees (and if I've been reading her signals at all correctly she probably will unless she's seeing someone or just doing her job) then she's thereby saying she would like to exchange numbers. By agreeing that she would like to see me again, she's agreeing to the logistical legwork necessary to make that happen. So after she agrees, either with a nod, a smile, or a verbal agreement, I pull out my phone, take her number, and then hit "call" so she has my number as well.

Don't get caught up in the details, though. The most important thing is, as always, the feeling. As I mentioned, the world is changing, and I can't count the number of times women have asked for my number because the feeling in the moment was that we both wanted to see each other again. As long as you're both communicating with that vibe and not suppressing those feelings (in your body or verbally), you'll probably see each other again -- the number exchange is just an afterthought.

SPEAKING ABOUT SEX SERIOUSLY

When the topic of sexuality arises in a conversation, a natural tension will arise over the interaction as well. Many times we look to diffuse this tension through humor or making some joke, but as I've already stated, a woman wants a man who can hold that tension without flinching. A woman will often make a sexual joke or allusion, and although she's probably not testing you purposefully, you will be judged on how you respond.

If she makes a joke about threesomes, it's ok to laugh at her joke. But if you become uncomfortable and try to make a bad joke or change the topic, she'll know that the topic of sex is one with which you're uncomfortable. As a result, she won't feel comfortable proceeding further down that road with you. If you treat the topic seriously, not giggling over your fantasy but instead expressing genuine interest, then you'll demonstrate that, despite the awkwardness surrounding the topic in our society, you're comfortable with that tension, and she can trust going there with you more.

It's the same as sexual innuendo, which also raises the tension of an interaction. When you're connected to your sexual energy and feeling sexual, the words that pop into your mind to use will naturally be more sexual in nature. When you're feeling sexual and speaking in a slower, more sexual tone, your communication will necessarily be laden with more sexual innuendo. If you try to force the innuendo by over-thinking, or chuckle it off with an over-the-top comment such as, "Huh huh, get it? *nudge, nudge*" then your attempt will come off as forced and awkward.

One note about speaking explicitly about more sexual topics; I'll wait for her or our physical actions to go there first. If she introduces a sexual topic I'll be as explicit as I can be on that topic (which is pretty explicit). If she tries to call you out for this explicitness you can remind her that she's the one who took the conversation there. I won't bring up oral sex before it happens, but afterward I'll explicitly state how I can't wait to do it again.

***

Sexual communication starts and ends with the sexual feelings in the moment, reflected in your body. **The second you disconnect from them and jump back into your head, look away, or try to force it, is the same second in which you lose the sexual connection.** That feeling must be communicated first through your body, and then through your words. If you don't, when she doesn't make the move for you you'll be wondering what could have been. Do so slowly, conscious of the other person's boundaries, and then continue to let nature take its course as far as you both actively enjoy it.

Every human being is entitled to express his or her sexuality with consensual partners. If you're repressing the natural sexuality in your communications with others or expressing it anxiously, then you're missing a major aspect of human interaction and signaling to everyone else that you're not comfortable with all of yourself. The underlying frustrations you've been experiencing have let you know that something was off.

It's time to remove the layers of fear and shame surrounding this God-given part of ourselves and start expressing ourselves the way that nature intended. It's time for you to start letting the women in your life know they can feel comfortable sharing their sexuality with you by having the courage to enjoy your own without agenda. I've given you the tools -- it's time for you to take the first steps forward.

Principle 13: Speaking Sexually is Simply Verbalizing, "You Turn Me On"

SECTION FOUR

The Missing Piece

CHAPTER 14

The Biggest Secret of All

These days we get pulled in a million different directions. Work often consumes our lives, sometimes to the point of insanity. Our physical health is typically on the low end of our priorities even though it's the one thing we can't get back. And our social life often seems to be at odds with our health when it's more about blowing off steam than connecting with others.

When we do get a smidge of free time, we watch TV, play video games, or do anything to give our brain a quick break from our near constant responsibilities. All the while we never take a moment to think about what's going on around us, and as we get older, life passes by faster and faster.

A simple thing that is easy to forget is that this is all connected. Guys often focus on their social skills when they want to improve their social life, forgetting that their physical and professional health are integral parts of that as well. And the healthier you are, mentally and physically, the more successful you'll be professionally and socially.

With so many things to focus on, it's easy to get side-tracked. That's why it's important to have balance in our lives. Specifically, there are four areas in our lives that must be given equal priority: your physical health, developing your purpose, spiritual health, and intimacy with others. If any of them begins to suffer from lack of attention, all of them will suffer.

PHYSICAL HEALTH

You only get one body and one life. The stronger your physical body, the more energy you'll have to put toward work -- and anything else you love -- and the more sound you'll be mentally and emotionally. The benefits also extend to your social life as well. Not only will you have more energy to socialize, but the stronger your body, the more you'll be able to hold space, process your feelings, and be comfortable with the feelings of the moment. When I'm fatigued I can't bring my best self to socializing and all of my interactions suffer.

The biggest determinant to your physical health is the amount of sleep you get (certainly tied to everything else on this list), and then comes exercise and diet. I'm not an exercise or diet coach, and I won't pretend that what works for me works for everyone. Any book you find in amazon's bestseller lists have been pre-screened as providing quality info. There's plenty of quality free to inexpensive resources available online. What's important is that you take action.

DEVELOPING YOUR PURPOSE

I believe that every single human being on the planet has an amazing gift to share with the rest of the world. It's our duty in life to discover, develop, and use that gift to benefit as many people as possible. Maybe we're afraid to fail in this area or we're not sure where to turn. We do the minimum we have to in order to get by, all the while telling ourselves we're somehow cheating the system. But the only thing we're cheating is ourselves. You'll realize it, at least subconsciously, in the stagnant mediocrity of your life, frustratedly knowing you were meant for something greater. Until you get your life on the path you were meant for, you'll only take that frustration out on yourself and everyone around you.

What do you love to do? Love the outdoors? There are plenty of careers in that area. Want to make a positive difference in the world? The possibilities are endless. Love numbers and spreadsheets? Fortunately your passions match up with what society has deemed most valuable. For those whose passions lie elsewhere, don't listen to what anyone else says you should be doing. At the end of the day there's only what makes you happy and fulfills you, and at the end of your life that's all that will matter. Hell, if a kid from Detroit can be a dating coach, you can do anything.

SPIRITUAL HEALTH

It doesn't matter what you believe in, what religion speaks most strongly to you -- if any religion at all. You can believe in an all-powerful being, or simply believe in the power of nature and the human spirit. What's important is that you take time off to rest and replenish yourself.

Meditation, in all of its forms, is simply the practice of quieting down your mind and getting more in touch with the feelings in your body. In terms used here, meditation is practicing holding space with yourself. If you're having trouble holding space with others, meditation (and exercise) should jump to the top of your list of priorities. The specific form you choose doesn't really matter, as long as you feel more peaceful and focused afterward and the near-constant stream of thoughts inside our heads have quieted down. Start with whatever form speaks most strongly to you.

Yoga is an excellent way to improve your spiritual health. This could easily be slotted under physical health, as it's certainly great for that, but I wanted to strongly distinguish between most western varieties of yoga -- which are essentially glorified cardio classes -- and yoga as it was traditionally practiced. At its core, yoga is about moving your body in specific ways to evoke different feelings so that they can be experienced. In this way it's another form of meditation.

There are many other ways to improve your spiritual health as well. Go for a walk in nature; go for a swim in the ocean. Look up at the sky and marvel at its vast infinity. Dump all of your problems onto someone else (therapists are great for this, lest you scare away friends). Clear your mind of the worries and stresses of the world and just take some time to relax and enjoy something you love. Life goes by quickly. It's up to you to slow it down.

INTIMACY

I could spend an entire chapter discussing scientific studies such as Ed Diener and Martin E.P. Seligman's 2002 study, "Very Happy People," which conclude that a person's happiness and overall well-being is more closely tied to the quality of his relationships than any other factor. A quick google search will provide an almost endless list of them. What may be more surprising is "Rat Park," a study published in 1980 by Bruce K. Alexander that highlighted the quality of our social lives -- or lack thereof -- as the main root of addiction. While my career makes me a bit biased in the belief that your relationships are the most important factor in your life (other than your body still functioning at a relatively healthy level), I fortunately have decades of scientific evidence to back me up.

My own personal hypothesis after working as a dating coach for over ten years is that when a person feels lonely and wants a romantic connection to fill the emptiness in his life, what he's really missing is intimacy with other human beings. It doesn't matter how many surface-level romantic relationships they have, if you're not developing true intimacy with others that emptiness will always persist.

Intimacy isn't solely determined by the amount of time spent with another person, but also by the quality of that time. Intimacy blossoms when people open themselves up and share things that make them feel uncomfortable. Conversations in which you share the things of which you're most ashamed with people you trust are great for this, but you open yourself up with someone else when you're simply having a great time enjoying their company. It's important to have both in your life.

Don't feel like there's anyone you can trust with your deepest secrets? Again, paying a professional to listen to those things in a secure setting, otherwise known as therapy, is a common first step. The more we keep those things to ourselves though, the more it reinforces the idea that we're unlovable and unworthy of closeness to others. The more we share these things and see that we won't be pushed away, the more we feel as though we do deserve deeper connections with others.

Have you moved away from your college friends and need to branch out from the office crowd? Fortunately there is a bonus chapter on making friends at any age.

***

These four elements make up a complete man, a complete human being. They are all of equal priority. If one suffers, they all suffer. Often when you're feeling "empty," scrambling to find something superficial to fill that void, it's because one or more of these aspects has been neglected. Take this moment right now to give yourself a self-evaluation. What areas do you over-prioritize, what areas are you lacking. By finding balance in these facets, we can reach our fullest potential in all of them and truly live the life we were meant to live.

Principle 14: Social Skills Are a Major Part of Your Happiness, But They're Not Enough

----

CHAPTER 15

The Last (And Most Important) Lesson

Most of the time after a coaching program, my alums go on to live happy social and dating lives and I don't hear much from them except pictures and stories of their girlfriends, invites to their weddings, or when they choose to pay what they've learned forward and help guys who were in the same place they used to be.

Sometimes though, a guy requires a bit of follow-up coaching (which I'm always more than happy to provide) in order to get them to that place. What I've found is that there is one main difference between the guys who have immediate success and the guys who need to work at it a bit longer, and if you take one thing away from this book it should be this:

The clients who quickly go onto live the social and dating lives of their dreams look at everything I've taught them -- everything you've learned in this book -- as a way to improve themselves and their relationships with everyone they come into contact with. The guys who still struggle a bit look at this very same information as a way to get some positive validation from a woman they're attracted to or put their success or failure on how single they are at that moment. They see a woman they're attracted to and apply everything they've learned to attempt to get her to like him, to get a positive reaction from her, to get her phone number, to hook up with her, to get her into a relationship -- and they base their opinion of themselves on their ability to do so.

You can always tell if a salesperson is more worried about their commission check than providing you excellent service. Even if they say all the right things, they give off this desperate, needy vibe that makes you feel a little disgusting inside.

Women are experts at knowing if a man is approaching her with something jumping around in the back of his head, even if he says all the right things. She might talk to the guy because she's bored, give her number out to be polite, or even hook up with the guy because she just wanted to get laid. The guy will then pat himself on the back for his seductive skills, but when she never meets up with him for a date it's because she felt that same disgust inside.

There's few things that are a bigger turnoff to women than guys who are out at the bar desperately prowling for affection. At the same time, there are few things women in a social situation find more attractive than guys who are genuinely enjoying their friends' company and the company of those around them. If you're desperately searching for a partner, you'll scare away anyone who catches a whiff of that desperation. It's when you focus on becoming the best person you can be that someone amazing will come along.

The guy who gets nervous and falls into the rut of trying to achieve a particular outcome isn't trying to be manipulative, of course. We've been raised in a culture that tells us over and over again that our value as men is at least partially dependent on our ability to attract a woman and that ultimate happiness comes from finding a partner. Many of us have had negative experience with women growing up -- or recently -- that have left us with bleeding insecurities when it comes to them. Expressing and experiencing our sexuality and intimacy in general is a natural part of life. When that part of ourselves is

111

starved it can be extremely difficult not to get nervous and fall into ruts.

Additionally, according to neuroscience, it's far more ingrained than that. When an environmental stimulus such as meeting new people causes feelings to arise in your body, these feelings send signals to the brain, beginning in the sensory cortex near the back of your brain, and from there head first to the limbic system -- the parts of your brain that regulate a wide range of processes including emotion, fear, memory, pleasure, and muscle behavior. It's not until moments later that these signals reach the part of your brain that deals with reasoning and critical thinking! For someone trying to stay present and not jump into his head, this is the worst possible combination. Within the first moments of noticing another person, you immediately assess, based on past experiences, how a potential interaction with that person might go. If they remind us of someone who hurt us, the amygdala is triggered and the feeling that washes over us is fear. If we determine that the person has the potential to bring us happiness, whatever that looks like for us, the nucleus accumbens (our brain's pleasure center) fires and our brain is flooded with dopamine. Suddenly, this person is the source of all happiness for us in the world (and then we probably worry about messing it up based on past experiences). The entire time, our heart rate, muscle behavior, and balance are all being affected by this rush of neurotransmitters.

It's literally impossible not to respond this way if you're a human being with a brain similar to 99.9% of the rest of us. The difference though, between the guys who are happy and the guys who still struggle, is how quickly these thoughts/feelings are processed by the frontal lobe, the home of higher-level reasoning. The frontal lobe gives us the ability to take all of the available input -- and make the best overall decision.

It typically takes about twice as long for information to reach the frontal lobe from the sensory cortex compared to the limbic system. For some of us, this process can take a lot longer. We get overwhelmed by the reactions from these other parts of the brain and our thoughts flee to the well worn neural pathways of dismissing these feelings/running away, obsessing over how great it would be to have this other person in your life to some capacity, or compulsively trying make that happen. Our bodies send off all of these signals, and the idea that we're unattractive is reinforced.

The good news is that these old neural pathways can be rewired. Science has shown that as we practice new habits, our brain physically changes by creating new neural pathways and weakening the less used ones. These new paths will become faster and more automatic to us the more we use them, and the less those old paths are used, the less likely you'll be to fall into them for longer periods of time.

When you encounter someone who unleashes a flood of chemicals in your brain, you can acknowledge that you feel afraid, or turned on. You can acknowledge that your brain is doing that typical brain thing where it either makes excuses for why you should run or realizing the potential "reward" there and getting over-excited about how to achieve it. With full consciousness of these things you can then say, "I realize I'm having these thoughts and feelings and they're perfectly normal and natural, the more I embrace these feelings, the more I'll probably enjoy this interaction. I also know that lingering on the thoughts created by these feelings won't do me any good, so I'll let them go and bring my attention back to enjoying connecting with this person in the moment." In other words, by practicing awareness and staying in the moment, you will teach your brain to create a "shortcut" whereby your frontal lobe will be able to react much faster to whatever is causing your limbic system to go haywire.

When you're "on", socially, whether it be for a night or a few weeks, it's because your brain started making this connection to the frontal lobe more quickly for some reason. You had all of the same thoughts you always do: "wow, she's pretty, I would like to be very close to her, her body looks amazing in that dress, I wonder if she's like me, I wonder if there's anything I can do to make her like me more." The times you're in the zone though, you don't linger on the thoughts, you don't really care about them as much as enjoying the moment as much as possible and feeling all of the feelings that might potentially come up.

For most of your lives, this frontal lobe shortcut happened subconsciously. When it stops happening the next morning a few weeks later, guys will scramble to get it back, wondering what they were saying or what they were doing, looking for the answer in all the places they're least likely to find it. Now that we are conscious of this process we can develop this superhighway to the frontal lobe with everyone we come into contact with. The more people respond positively to us as we do, the stronger and more automatic this neural pathway becomes, and the faster your old ruts disappear as the neural pathways that fed them shrink. You'll still have points in your life where you fall into them, this is natural, but the more you build up this new pathway the easier it is to stay on course and be "on" all the time.

As you try to improve at this when you encounter someone who intimidates you, you'll naturally fall back into your old ruts. This "failure" can be discouraging, but it's no different than Michael Jordan and Lebron James struggling in their first several trips to the playoffs. The first times we attempt something difficult in an environment that already makes us nervous, the more difficult it will be not to fall into a rut and choke. The more we practice the fundamentals -- in their case dribbling, shooting, and keeping your eye on the ball, in ours, holding space, enjoying others' company, and expressing our sexuality without anxiety or agenda -- in situations that aren't as intimidating, the better shot we'll have of doing it when our heart is beating out of our chest. The first several times we attempt to put our best selves forward in those tough situations, just like those star athletes, we'll probably choke. As they did though, you can see this situation as an opportunity to become aware of how your ruts affect you in these circumstances and learn to do everything you've practiced while embracing them.

It's also much easier not to fall into the rut of trying to control the outcome when we remember that her response isn't personal. We often desire a positive response from that person to whom we're attracted because we feel that our own value, at least in part, depends on their response to us. It's not that she wasn't in the mood to talk at that moment, it's that she thought I was weird. It's not that she didn't like the smell of my sweat, that she wasn't in a sexual mood at the moment, or that I wasn't comfortable expressing my own sexuality -- it's that I'm an unattractive person. This just reaffirms everything I learned about myself in middle school.

If someone is attracted to you, it's because you put yourself out there, they were in the mood to socialize at that moment, they liked the smell of your sweat (and all the other little biological factors that are subconsciously communicated), and neither of you sabotaged the natural process of connection with one of the many ruts highlighted in this book. If someone's not attracted to you or doesn't respond to you with warmth, it might be because one of your ruts spoiled the interaction (and you received an excellent learning experience because you put yourself out there). Or it might be they simply weren't in the mood to talk, they had a boyfriend, or there was some other reason that had nothing to do with you. The guys I coach who go on to live happy and fulfilling social and dating lives don't worry about the response when they say "hi," to a stranger, they simply do their best to stay as present with their feelings as possible while expressing them, avoid their own ruts, and enjoy the moment however it ends up.

The secret to being an attractive person is to not try to attract people. Attraction is a force of nature, not a force of will. Deeper attraction will naturally happen if you start conversations with your only goal being to express your feelings in the moment while feeling where the other person is at, have conversations with the goal of enjoying them and building intimacy, and flirt with the goal of enjoying the beautiful, God-given feelings of sexuality. Keep working on your ability to do so in all interactions, and become more aware of how you deviate when you care most about the interaction, and you can overcome this rut as well.

Getting laid is easy. Being happy is a practice. Practice connecting with others every day, everywhere you go, while being vulnerable with your feelings, and it won't be long before you're living the social and dating life you've always dreamed of.

Principle 15: Don't Try to Attract Someone, Focus on Becoming Your Most Attractive Self

----

Conclusion

Up until you were about eighteen, you didn't choose this life. You didn't choose to grow up in a culture where we interact with strangers more out of fear than out of love, where education on communication is limited to the benefits of "active listening," and where men and women are segregated and at early age and told how different they are. You didn't choose to live in a society where this lack of knowledge results in us trying to all figure it out for ourselves amid the confusion of mixed-messages from the media, and where far too much hurt, confusion, and animosity has developed between men and women because of this limited education despite us all just trying to do our best.

Tony didn't choose to be in a wheelchair, and Adam didn't choose to be blind, yet they had a choice nonetheless. They could have settled for the world the way it was, for everyone telling them what their limits were and how they ought to act. Tony and Adam, however, didn't want to settle for that and because they chose to break those barriers, everyone who has the pleasure of knowing them and seeing their courage is better off for it.

Our brain creates excuses because it's trying to protect us from that which we fear. Sometimes, those concerns are very valid. For example, "I shouldn't get into that tiger cage because I might get eaten," is a very valid excuse.

When it comes to socializing and women though, the fears you have are tied to vulnerabilities of your youth that have long since hardened. Or your fears have been fed to you through society and the media and don't have basis in reality. When examined, the excuses you make in light of these fears don't hold water.

You now know that "rejection" isn't personal, it can provide a valuable learning experience and/or has nothing to do with you whatsoever. You know that blaming your conversational woes on "not knowing what to say" is merely a way your brain avoids the real fear of holding the tension in an interaction with someone and creating real intimacy. You now know that you can only lose a potential romantic connection by suppressing your desire -- not by expressing it.

Excuses and rationalizations can provide us peace of mind. If your excuse is, "I don't know what I'm doing (or I can't find the time and the resources) so I can't do it" -- it can provide a convenient buffer to actually doing the tough work that you don't want to do. Now that these excuses have been removed, the only thing you're left with is a decision.

Reading a book on fitness and going to the gym once won't get you six-pack abs. In order to achieve the benefits of that knowledge you have to decide to take action. You can decide not to eat healthy and not exercise regularly, and sometimes in life we have to dedicate our limited resources to improving other areas of our lives. But at the same time you can't complain about being out of shape or that "women only like guys who are fit" because you chose that path consciously.

In the same way, now that you know exactly how to achieve the kind of social and dating life that you desire, if you ever feel lonely or unsatisfied with the way things are going for you, you can't complain because you made the decision to embrace that life when you decided not to take the steps that you knew would change your situation.

I'm not saying it'll be easy. The actions I prescribe should make you feel uncomfortable -- especially around the people who intimidate you the most -- because you're not used to doing them and because they fly in the face of some deeply rooted fears and cultural education you've received. But if you want a different outcome you have to take different actions. Thus, more often than not it's the case that the more you feel uncomfortable at first, the more you're doing it right. Once you start getting those positive reactions from other people though, that's when you start to feel more comfortable in those situations. That's when it becomes natural.

It's not easy. Self-development never is. I'm just saying that you have a choice. You can accept your world as it is or you can change the landscape. You can choose to practice these actions with every single person you come into contact with, or you can go on "autopilot" in your interactions and reinforce the actions that got you here in the first place.

You can have a more fulfilling social life, go on more dates, make more friends, find a lifelong partner, improve the quality of your workplace relationships, and discover just how much your professional development depends on your social skills when your income jumps to where it should be ... whatever you truly desire. This isn't just about women, this is about living the potential life you have available versus settling for an alternate path dictated by your fears.

Most people take the easier path and do just fine with their lives, never really knowing what was possible. Few among us push ourselves to reach our full potential, and while we celebrate the accomplishments of those who do, our society rarely focuses on the work that went into attaining them. Make no mistake about it though, at one point in time those individuals faced similar fears and hardships, and chose to take the more difficult path.

Once again, it won't be easy and I promise that you'll want to give up more than once. You're going to have bad days where no one seems to show you any warmth. I believe these days when you're seduced by your old demons and fall back into your old ruts are put there to test your resolve. It's when times are tough that we find the true measure ourselves.

Like I've said to every one of my potential clients, I can only show you the path, you have to be the one who walks it. No one can make that choice for you, but it would genuinely be a shame if you didn't realize your full potential. Your friends, colleagues, and family (present and future) would be missing out on the man that they deserve. More importantly, you'll be missing out on the friends, professional development, family, and overall life that you deserve.

You didn't choose the world in which you were raised, but you can choose to create the world in which you live. By removing the self-imposed limits on yourself and embracing real connection with others you'll meet friends and girlfriends you never would have otherwise. At the same time, you'll get exposed to new thoughts and experiences you never would have found, and introduce friends who never would have had the pleasure of knowing each other.

Give people the space to open up and show their amazing-ness in conversation while being vulnerable and you'll start to surprise yourself with how many compelling people with similar interests you'll find. Expressing sexuality is a concept met with confusion and shame for both men and women. But by having the courage to comfortably express your sexuality without agenda you'll show her that she can forget the lessons society has taught her and feel safe and sexy in expressing hers.

It won't happen overnight, but the more women leave our company with an amazing experience, the more we'll erode that animosity that exists between us that leads to so much hurt and frustration on both sides and the closer we'll get to living in the sort of dating utopia that we all want.

Right now there's a generation of kids who don't have to grow up facing the same pain and struggle that we faced, who can walk up to someone and express their feelings without fear. We may not be ready for this book to be introduced into classrooms just yet, but it starts with the basic lessons being applied in our own lives and passed on to the people that we meet. It may sound like a dream to some, but I believe it's possible, and I hope that you join me in helping to make it a reality.

In a Nutshell

Principle 1: Hold Space With Everyone and Identify Your Ruts

Principle 2: Make Socializing a Habit and Get Your Social Momentum Rolling ASAP

Principle 3: Communication Starts Before Words are Ever Spoken

Principle 4: Say Whatever's on Your Mind to Whomever's Around You

Principle 5: Destroy Rejection With The Warm Goodbye

Principle 6: It's Better to Be Interested Than Interesting

Principle 7: Enjoy Connecting with People & Go With Your First Instinct

Principle 8: Fill Silences With Genuine Interest And Allow Her to Share the Responsibility

Principle 9: Let Your Body Go & Unlock the Full Potential of Your Interactions

Principle 10: Instead of Trying to Win Her Over, Confidently Express Your Feelings

Principle 11: Flirt with Everyone by Expressing Your Sexuality with Your Whole Body

Principle 12: Sex Happens, Not When You Make It Happen, but When You Let It Happen

Principle 13: Speaking Sexually is Simply Verbalizing, "You Turn Me On"

Principle 14: Social Skills Are a Major Part of Your Happiness, But They're Not Enough

Principle 15: Don't Try to Attract Someone, Focus on Becoming Your Most Attractive Self

Acknowledgements

Aside from my alums, there are a few individuals I have to thank for helping to make this book a reality:

First and foremost to my friend and mentor, Jonathan Christian Hudson: Thank you for taking a chance on a kid with a dream from the Midwest, nurturing my coaching career, teaching me everything I know about this industry, and always believing in me. I wouldn't be here without you.

To my professional soulmate, Christina Berkley: Thank you for being such a tremendously positive influence on my personal and professional development, for being such a great friend, and for being the amazing person you are.

To all of my assistants, past and present: Thank you for helping to make my coaching programs so special.

To my parents and grandparents: Thank you for your unwavering support despite my unconventional career path.

To Joseph Romm: Thank you for helping me turn a rough draft into a book and teaching me how to be a writer.

To Tessla Coil: Thank you for sharing your insight into the human condition and talent for writing -- and for providing a perfect title to this book.

To Fran Rengel: Thank you for generously donating your time and talent to the introduction.

To Phil Drazewski and Ryan Cockerill: Thank you for making me believe that this crazy dream was possible, and that I was capable of doing it.

To every woman I've ever dated and/or been friends with: Thank you for teaching me everything I know about women -- especially that we're far more alike than different.

To every woman I've ever loved: Thank you for inspiring me to be my best self, helping to show me what I couldn't see on my own, and most of all, for loving me.

Bonus Section Five

The Most Commonly Asked Follow-up Questions

Available online at www.sparksofattraction.com/bonus-chapters

If you enjoyed this book, write a review!

If you enjoyed this book, it would mean a lot to me if you would please take a moment to write an honest review on Amazon at http://www.amazon.com/gp/product/B01680KDA2 and share what you learned and how it has helped you so that others can discover this same valuable information. I strongly believe that this information will help change people's lives, and you can help too by sharing your experiences with others. Thank you!

****

CPSIA information can be obtained at www.ICGtesting.com
Printed in the USA
BVOW06s1756090416

443648BV00011B/25/P